INTERNATIONAL DEVELOPMENT IN FOCUS

Recycling of Used Lead-Acid Batteries

Guidelines for Appraisal of Environmental Health Impacts

KATHERINE VON STACKELBERG, PAMELA R. D. WILLIAMS,
ERNESTO SÁNCHEZ-TRIANA, SANTIAGO ENRIQUEZ, AND CLAUDIA SERRANO

WORLD BANK GROUP

Contents

Boxes

Figures

Tables

Acknowledgments

The background research and drafts for this report were prepared by Katherine von Stackelberg and Pamela Williams. The task team included Montserrat Meiro-Lorenzo, Gabriela Elizondo, Maria Rosa Puech, Lek Gjon Kadeli, Mayra Guerra Lopez, Claudia Serrano, Santiago Enriquez, and Ernesto Sánchez-Triana (Task Team Leader). Frank Van Woerden, A. S. Harinath, and Shafick Hoossein were peer reviewers for this analytical work. Editorial support was provided by Stan Wanat (Stanford University).

This analytical work was supervised by Karin Kemper (Global Director, Environment, Natural Resources and Blue Economy Global Practice—ENB), and Iain Shuker and Christian Peter (Practice Managers, Global Platform Unit, ENB). This analytical work was funded by the Pollution Management and Environmental Health Multi-Donor Trust Fund (PMEH).

Executive Summary

Despite robust evidence documenting the tragic and widespread consequences of lead exposure, some environmental and health authorities around the world, particularly in low- and middle-income countries (LMICs), have yet to develop regulatory responses. The 2019 Global Burden of Disease (GBD 2019 Diseases and Injuries Collaborators 2020) report estimated that lead exposure resulted in more than 900,000 deaths and 21.7 million years of healthy life lost (measured in disability-adjusted life years, or DALYs) worldwide due to long-term effects of lead exposure on health. Since 1990, between 84 percent and 88 percent of the health impacts of lead exposure have occurred in lower-middle-income and upper-middle-income countries. These estimates likely represent an underestimation since they underestimate the full costs of lead exposure in that they do not include all endpoints. Notable among all such endpoints is the loss of IQ points in children.

The available evidence suggests that lead exposure represents a significant risk in most countries around the world. The US Centers for Disease Control and Prevention has determined that blood lead levels at or above 5 micrograms per deciliter are a threshold for regulatory action. Based on this criterion, it is estimated that 1 in 3 children, or approximately 800 million children, have high blood lead levels.

In low- and middle-income countries, small-scale informal industries are known to operate with little regulatory oversight. These small, informal operations routinely dispose of chemicals directly onto and into the land, water, and air, generating the potential for significant exposures and resulting health risks for workers and surrounding communities. The small scale of these operations may create a false perception that they are a minor concern; however, they significantly outnumber large operations across a number of market segments.

A primary obstacle in addressing chemical pollution, including lead exposure, is the uncertainty about the sources of chemical exposures and their relationships to health outcomes. Information on individual exposure factors and behaviors contributing to exposure is typically lacking, having traditionally been collected for high-income countries (HICs), which may not be reliable or accurate for assessing exposures in LMICs.

The general guidelines presented in this report provide a pragmatic framework for designing representative studies and developing uniform sampling guidelines to support estimates of morbidity that are explicitly linked to exposure to land-based contaminants from used lead-acid battery (ULAB) recycling activities. A primary goal is to support environmental burden of disease evaluations, which attempt to attribute health outcomes to specific sources of pollution. The guidelines provide recommendations on the most appropriate and cost-effective sampling and analysis methods to ensure the collection of representative population-level data. Additionally, the guidelines will provide sample-size recommendations for each contaminant, as well as environmental media, biological sampling data, household-survey data, and health-outcome data.

These guidelines focus on small-scale ULABs that are known to generate significant amounts of lead waste through the smelting process, as well as other metal waste, including arsenic and cadmium. A primary concern with lead exposures is the documented association with neurodevelopmental outcomes in children, as demonstrated by statistically significantly reduced performance on a battery of cognitive tests. These associations are evident even in the youngest children, and toxicological and epidemiologic data indicate these effects have no threshold (that is, there is no safe level of exposure). Other potential exposures include arsenic and cadmium, and exposure to these contaminants is also associated with neurodevelopmental outcomes in children, as well as arsenicosis; bladder, lung, and skin cancers; and renal outcomes.

The primary objective of these guidelines is to guide research to assess the relationship between environmental contamination, exposures, and health outcomes related to a subset of contaminants originating from ULAB activities for particularly vulnerable populations, such as children, and the general population within a single household in the vicinity of ULAB sites in LMICs. To achieve this objective, biomonitoring and health-outcome data are linked to household-survey data and environmental data (for example, soil, dust, water, agricultural products, fish) at the individual level from an exposed population compared to individuals from an unexposed (reference) population. Data on exposures and health outcomes in the same individual, across a representative set of individuals, is required to support an understanding of the potential impact of ULAB activities on local populations. The guidelines can also assist in building local capacity to conduct environmental assessments following a consistent methodology to facilitate comparability across ULAB sites in different geographic areas. Sampling strategies and methods are prioritized given information needs, resource availability, and other constraints or considerations. The guidelines include a number of supporting appendixes, where additional resources and references on relevant topics can be found.

The *Conceptual Site Model (CSM)* provides a qualitative, graphical overview of the relationship between sources of contaminants, migration of contaminants through the environment, exposure pathways, and health outcomes. Figure ES.1 provides a general conceptual site model for ULAB activities. The CSM demonstrates how contaminants that are released, emitted, or discharged from ULAB sources can migrate through the environment, depending on local conditions. The CSM also demonstrates the pathways and routes by which individuals in the population can be exposed. This general CSM provides the starting point for developing a site-specific CSM.

Problem formulation is the process of (a) establishing study objectives, (b) supporting the identification of data-quality objectives associated with statistical analyses, and (c) developing a strategy. The objective of the strategy is to characterize the zone of influence or community footprint associated with ULAB activities in a specific geographic area. A detailed checklist is provided to (a) assist in developing a land-use map of the area and to (b) refine the general CSM for the site of interest based on existing site-specific information and knowledge.

To meet the primary research objective, the *sampling design* is structured to link environmental contamination and individual exposures to multiple contaminants of concern (CoCs) with different health outcomes associated with exposure to these CoCs at the household level. Selected households and sampling locations should therefore provide data on *how* environmental contamination contributes to household exposures. The process of identifying local hotspots or fully characterizing environmental concentrations across the entire site will likely require a different sampling strategy. These guidelines recommend a primary grid-based sampling-design strategy augmented by targeted sampling where individuals spend significant amounts of time (for example, schools, playgrounds, agricultural locations). Typical grid densities range from 20 x 20 m to 100 x 100 m, with most falling generally in the 40 x 40 m to 60 x 60 m range. A household is selected from each grid node with an example provided.

Recommendations for a *Home Survey Questionnaire* provide the detailed information on exposure factors. These factors include time-activity patterns, food-frequency questionnaires, and other demographic information. This information is used to link environmental sampling data with biomonitoring data and health-outcome data in a specific community. As these data are collected, they should be compiled into country- or region-specific databases. These databases can support development of risk assessments and other analyses that require quantifying exposure factors (for example, consumption rates, body weight, and so forth). Such quantification can be used to predict, for example, contaminant-specific intake rates applicable to analyses for pollution sources beyond ULAB facilities.

Media-specific *environmental sampling* recommendations are provided as follows:

Soil

- Collect four individual soil samples and analyze for metals using in-field X-ray fluorescence (XRF).
- Composite the samples and send them to a laboratory for a multi-metal screen.
- If resources allow, 50 percent of household samples—randomly selected—and 100 percent of targeted samples undergo bioavailability testing for Pb.

Dust

- Collect two individual dust samples from interior surfaces using an appropriate wipe (for example, GhostWipe™) and analyze using in-field XRF.
- Composite the samples and send to an accredited laboratory for a multi-metal screen.

xii | RECYCLING OF USED LEAD-ACID BATTERIES

Water

- Water samples should be collected at the point of release at the individual household or dwelling where the water is available for consumption or use, unless there is a communal water source (for example, a community well or common surface water).
- Samples can also be collected directly from an off-site surface-water body if it is commonly used for recreational or other purposes (or if the in-field research team requires additional data on potential site contamination).
- Collect 1-liter samples and send to an accredited laboratory for a multi-metal screen.

Agricultural products

- The household survey and food-frequency questionnaire should inform the selection of specific items being collected, with an emphasis on composite samples that reflect dietary items for the largest number of participating households.
- Agricultural samples can include meat, dairy (including processed items such as cheese), eggs, fruits, and vegetables, and should be collected from the point of consumption (for example, kitchen), garden, or market, as determined by the in-field team.
- Collect somewhere between 40 and 100 grams of biomass, depending on specific laboratory guidance.

Individuals from participating households provide *biomonitoring* and *health-outcome* data. These are related as shown in table ES.1.

FIGURE ES.1

General conceptual site model of sources for health outcomes at ULAB sites

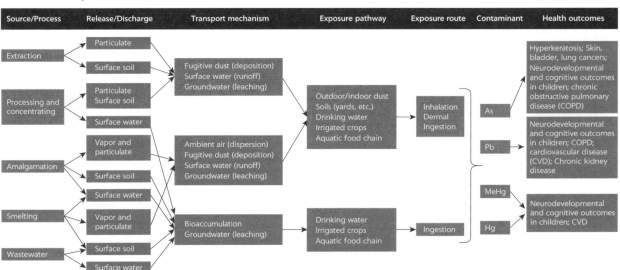

TABLE ES.1 **Summary of biomonitoring and health-outcome measurement recommendations**

CoC	BIOMARKER OF EXPOSURE	HEALTH OUTCOMES AND BIOMARKERS OF EFFECT
arsenic (As)	Gold standard is metabolite monomethylarsonic acid (%MMA) obtained from a speciated creatinine-adjusted urine sample	• Conduct age-specific, culturally relevant cognitive testing for each child. • Conduct in-field screening for keratosis on the soles of the feet as part of the household survey or as part of a more formal medical examination. • If keratosis is observed, consider a carcinogenic biomarker, such as DNA adduct assay or micronucleus formation assay. • Measure C-reactive protein as a nonspecific biomarker of intermediate effects on the renal and cardiovascular systems.
cadmium (Cd)	International consensus on use of creatine-adjusted urine	• Measure sensitive urinary biomarkers, including β2-m (urinary β2-microglobulin) and glomerular filtration rate (GfR). • If elevated, consider measuring additional carcinogenic biomarkers, such as DNA adduct formation or micronucleus formation.
lead (Pb)	Venous blood is the gold standard; dried capillary blood spot using in-field LeadCare Analyzer	• Measure blood pressure in adults in the field or as part of a medical examination. • Measure specific biomarkers including proteinuria (for example, albumin); anemia status (for example, hematocrit); cardiovascular risk (for example, C-reactive protein); ALA for Pb exposures. • Conduct age-specific, culturally relevant cognitive testing for each child.

Source: von Stackelberg, Williams, and Sánchez-Triana 2021.
Note: CoC = contaminant of concern.

CONCLUSIONS

Data obtained following these recommendations can be used to support consistent, comparable, and standardized community-risk and health-impact assessments at contaminated sites in LMICs. These data can also be used to support subsequent economic-burden analyses and risk-management decision-making with respect to site cleanup and risk-mitigation options in the most cost-effective and efficient manner. Adherence to this framework will facilitate comparisons and meta-analyses across studies by standardizing data-collection efforts at the community level.

REFERENCES

GBD (Global Burden of Disease) 2019 Diseases and Injuries Collaborators. 2020. "Global Burden of 369 Diseases and Injuries in 204 Countries and Territories, 1990–2019: A Systematic Analysis for the Global Burden of Disease Study 2019." *Lancet* 396 (10258): 1204–22. https://www.thelancet.com/journals/lancet/article/PIIS0140-6736(20)30925-9/fulltext.

von Stackelberg, Katherine, Pamela R. D. Williams, and Ernesto Sánchez-Triana. 2021. "A Systematic Framework for Collecting Site-Specific Sampling and Survey Data to Support Analyses of Health Impacts from Land-Based Pollution in Low- and Middle-Income Countries." *Int. J. Environ. Res. Public Health* 18: 4676. https://doi.org/10.3390/ijerph18094676.

Abbreviations

As	arsenic
ATSDR	Agency for Toxic Substances and Disease Registry
BLL	blood lead levels
Cd	cadmium
CDC	Centers for Disease Control and Prevention (US)
CoC	contaminant of concern
CSM	conceptual site model
DALY	disability-adjusted life year
GBD	Global Burden of Disease
HICs	high-income countries
ICP-MS	inductively coupled plasma mass spectrometry
LMICs	low- and middle-income countries
Pb	lead
PMEH	Pollution Management and Environmental Health
ULAB	used lead-acid battery
US EPA	United States Environmental Protection Agency
WHO	World Health Organization
XRF	X-ray fluorescence

1 Introduction

Despite robust evidence documenting the tragic and widespread consequences of lead exposure, many environmental and health authorities around the world, particularly in low- and middle-income countries (LMICs), have yet to develop regulatory responses. The issue has received little attention, perhaps because it has low visibility compared to other environmental issues. When water is contaminated, people become acutely ill with diarrhea and other symptoms that can lead to death. Similarly, poor air quality leads to overt symptoms and premature mortality. Exposure to environmental contaminants such as lead is associated with more insidious outcomes, such as reduced performance on cognitive tests and other neurological disorders.

Although exposure to lead can cause death and acute illnesses in individuals, the problem is more subtle for most-affected populations. Affected children do not perform as well in school. They are late to read. They are slow to learn how to perform common tasks. Perhaps a few more children are born with cognitive deficits. Perhaps these children have less impulse control. Perhaps they exhibit more violence. These symptoms are not always understood as an environmental or a public health issue—or indeed a development problem. Instead, people will say it is an issue of morals or of education. They will discipline the children, and then they will take themselves to task and ask how and why they are failing to raise these children correctly. It is not always clear that the issue may be an environmental exposure.

Historically, high lead levels were caused by lead in gasoline. The phaseout of leaded gasoline is in many ways a public health and environmental success story, but it may also have contributed to a false perception that lead is no longer a major environmental and health challenge. Outbreaks of childhood lead poisoning in low-, middle-, and high-income countries have occasionally surfaced in the news, generally documenting contamination from a nearby mine or smelter, creating the impression that lead exposure is a problem that affects only a few intermittent communities.

The 2019 Global Burden of Disease report (GBD 2019 Diseases and Injuries Collaborators 2020) estimated that lead exposure resulted in more than 900,000 deaths and 21.7 million years of healthy life lost (measured in disability-adjusted life years or DALYs) worldwide due to long-term effects of lead exposure on health. Lead exposure accounted for 62.5 percent of the global burden of idiopathic developmental intellectual disability, 8.2 percent of the global burden of hypertensive heart disease, 7.2 percent of the global burden of ischemic heart disease, and 5.6 percent of global burden of strokes (Murray et al. 2020).

Since 1990, between 84 percent and 88 percent of the health impacts of lead exposure have occurred in lower-middle- and upper-middle-income countries. Between 1990 and 2019, the health impacts of lead exposure grew by more than 35 percent globally, with LMICs experiencing rapid growth and high-income countries achieving a decline of more than 30 percent (figure 1.1). South Asia and East Asia and the Pacific are the regions where lead exposure has led to the largest number of predicted DALYs (see figure 1.2).

These figures demonstrate the significant health effects caused by lead exposure predicted by DALYs, which may underestimate the full costs of lead exposure because they do not explicitly include the loss of IQ points in children. The World Bank has conducted several studies to estimate the health effects and costs of environmental degradation, including lead exposure. Table 1.1 summarizes the results of the studies conducted in Argentina, Bolivia, Lao People's Democratic Republic (PDR), and Mexico. In all countries, lead exposure results in increased mortality and morbidity among adults, and in significant neuropsychological effects in children. In addition to the pain and suffering associated with these premature deaths and illnesses, lead exposure results in costs that represent a significant share of each country's GDP. The biggest share of this cost stems from the loss of IQ points.

Similar studies have also been conducted to estimate the health effects and costs of lead exposure at the subnational level, as summarized in table 1.2. These studies have addressed geographic areas with very different characteristics. What is consistent across all of them is that lead represents a significant health risk and causes significant economic costs.

FIGURE 1.1

Disability-adjusted life years caused by lead exposure by income level, 1990–2019

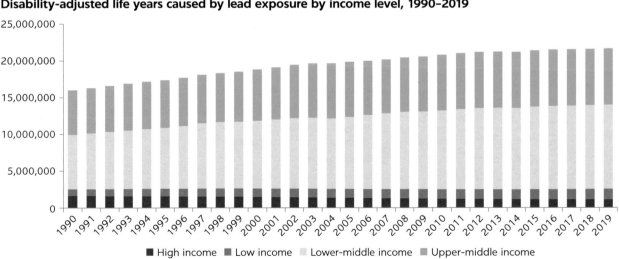

Source: Based on data from the GBD 2019.

FIGURE 1.2
Disability-adjusted life years caused by lead exposure by region, 1990–2019

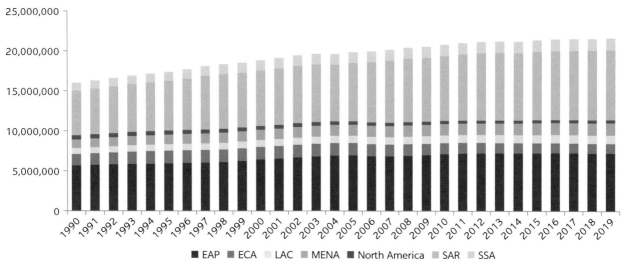

Source: Based on data from the GBD 2019.
Note: EAP = East Asia and Pacific region; ECA = Europe and Central Asia region; LAC = Latin America and the Caribbean region;
MENA = Middle East and Northern Africa region; SAR = South Asia region; SSA = Sub-Saharan Africa region.

TABLE 1.1 **Summary of national-level estimates of the cost of lead exposure**

COST MEASURE	ARGENTINA (2012)	BOLIVIA (2014)	LAO PDR (2017)	MEXICO (2018)
Total population (million)	41.1	11	6.86	126
GDP per capita (US$)	11,573	3,150	2,500	9,763
Labor force participation rate (15–64 years)	68%	74%	81%	65%
IQ points lost per year	619,581	345,576	341,615	3,838,340
Cost of IQ loss (% of GDP)	0.60%	1.35%	1.9%	0.97%
Annual deaths from adult lead exposure	2,082	371	562	5,105
Days of illness from adult lead exposure (million)	9.7	2.2	2.2	116
Cost of increased mortality and morbidity of adult lead exposure (% of GDP)	0.31%	0.21%	0.65%	0.39%
Total cost (% of GDP)	**0.91%**	**1.56%**	**2.55%**	**1.36%**

Source: World Bank compilation.

TABLE 1.2 **Summary of subnational-level estimates of the cost of lead exposure**

COST MEASURE	APURIMAC, PERU (2012)	SINDH, PAKISTAN (2009)	HIDALGO, MEXICO (2012)	YUCATÁN PENINSULA, MEXICO (2013)
Total population	452,000	36,000,000	2,800,000	4,300,000
GDP per capita (US$)	$1,931	$1,279	$6,980	$8,967
IQ points lost per year	11,200	1,984,840	55,200	142,000
Cost of IQ % of GDP, 2018	1.34%	2.54%	0.63%	1.14%
Annual deaths from adult lead exposure	11	—	63	138

continued

TABLE 1.2, *Continued*

COST MEASURE	APURIMAC, PERU (2012)	SINDH, PAKISTAN (2009)	HIDALGO, MEXICO (2012)	YUCATÁN PENINSULA, MEXICO (2013)
Days of illness from adult lead exposure	58,000	—	232,000	505,000
Cost of increased mortality and morbidity of adult lead exposure	0.15%	—	0.13%	0.18%
Total cost (% of GDP)	**1.49%**	**2.54%**	**0.76%**	**1.33%**

Source: World Bank compilation.
Note: — = not available.

Among the subnational areas included in these studies, lead had the highest costs in the Pakistani province of Sindh. There were multiple sources of lead exposure in Sindh at the time of the study, including drinking water. In a study of 18 districts of Karachi in 2007 and 2008, lead concentrations exceeded the World Health Organization (WHO) guideline limit of 10 micrograms per liter of water (µg/L) in 89 percent of the sampled sources. The average lead concentration was 77 µg/L in drinking water originating from surface sources and 146 µg/L in groundwater sources. Other potentially important sources of lead exposure included the traditional cosmetic surma, which often had a very high lead concentration of > 65 percent. Children's ornaments and jewelry often also contained lead (Sánchez-Triana et al. 2015).

Available evidence indicates that lead exposure represents a significant exposure and potential risk in most countries around the world. The US Centers for Disease Control and Prevention has determined that blood lead levels at or above 5 micrograms per deciliter is a cause for action. Based on this criterion, it is estimated that 1 in 3 children, or approximately 800 million children, have high lead blood levels (figure 1.3). What is even more worrisome is that scientific evidence is increasingly showing that there is no threshold blood lead level below which there are no impacts on children's health. That means that an even larger number of children could be at risk of being affected by lead exposure and the resulting health effects, which might include increased aggressive behavior, impulsivity, attention-deficit hyperactivity disorder (ADHD), and mild retardation, all of which are characteristics known to be associated with violent and criminal behavior.

The reduction in lead exposure observed in high-income countries has been associated with improved regulations and strict enforcement. However, in LMICs, environmental regulations are lacking. Moreover, while environmental enforcement agencies in LMICs may dedicate their limited resources to regulating the operations of larger polluting manufacturing operations, small-scale informal industries tend to operate without any form of regulatory supervision. These small, informal operations routinely dispose of chemicals directly onto and into land, water, and air, generating the potential for significant health risks for workers and surrounding communities. The small scale of these operations may create a false perception that they are a minor concern; however, they significantly outnumber large operations in a number of market segments.

A major obstacle in addressing chemical pollution, including lead exposure, is the uncertainty about sources of chemical-pollution exposures and their relationship to health outcomes. Exposure factors and behaviors contributing to exposures have traditionally been collected for high-income countries and may not be reliable or accurate for assessing exposures in low- and middle-income countries.

FIGURE 1.3

Children's average blood lead levels by country (µg/dl)

Lead (pollution)

Lead pollution
Average BLL (µg/dL)

15 5 3 2 1 0

Source: UNICEF/Pure Earth (2020), based on data from IHME (2019).
Note: BLL = blood lead level.

These general guidelines aim to overcome this obstacle by assisting field researchers in applying a consistent and uniform, yet flexible and practical, approach for information gathering and data collection across different used lead-acid battery (ULAB) recycling and reference sites in LMICs. The information and data obtained can be used to assess the relationship between environmental contamination generated by ULAB-recycling activities and individual-based biomonitoring and health-outcome data among the general population living near these sites, along with associated reference sites. The guidelines can also be used to assist in building local capacity to conduct environmental assessments following a consistent methodology to facilitate comparability across ULAB sites in different geographic areas. Sampling strategies are prioritized given information needs, resource availability, and other constraints or considerations. The guidelines include a number of supporting appendixes where additional resources and references on various topics can be found.

STRUCTURE OF THE REPORT

Chapter 2 of this report provides an overview of the ULAB-recycling process, including a description of the primary contaminants released or discharged during each step of the process. This chapter also presents a general conceptual site model (CSM) for ULAB-recycling sites that identifies the transport mechanisms, exposure pathways, and routes of exposure for local populations that may be exposed to these contaminants. Lastly, this chapter highlights key site-specific questions or issues that should be considered to inform the selection of participating households and sampling locations at ULAB-recycling sites.

Subsequent chapters of the guidelines provide guidance for information gathering and data collection during field implementation at the identified ULAB-recycling sites. Chapter 3 describes the process for identifying participating households and individuals within those households that will provide household-survey data (appendix B), environmental sampling data (chapter 4), biomonitoring data (chapter 5), and health-outcome data (chapter 6). This is a critical step that will determine where to conduct subsequent environmental sampling of soil, sediment, dust, water, fish, or agricultural and food products, and for whom to collect biological and health outcome data, in order to assess the potential contribution of ULAB-related contamination to population-level exposures and health outcomes in exposed individuals. Chapter 4 provides general guidelines for conducting environmental sampling of soil, dust, sediment, water, fish, and/or agricultural and food products. Chapter 5 provides general guidelines for collecting biological samples in blood, urine, hair, or other matrices. Chapter 6 provides general guidelines for evaluating health outcomes using medical exams, health surveys, and diagnostic tests.

The guidelines focus on data collection as opposed to data analysis. The choice of statistical models and analyses will depend on site-specific study objectives, the site-specific CSM, and the ultimate number of households and samples available.

REFERENCES

GBD (Global Burden of Disease) 2019 Diseases and Injuries Collaborators. 2020. "Global Burden of 369 Diseases and Injuries in 204 Countries and Territories, 1990–2019: A Systematic Analysis for the Global Burden of Disease Study 2019." *Lancet* 396 (10258): 1204–22. https://www.thelancet.com/journals/lancet/article/PIIS0140-6736(20)30925-9 /fulltext.

IHME (Institute for Health Metrics and Evaluation). 2019. "Global Burden of Disease Study Resources." http://www.healthdata.org/.

Murray, C. J., A. Y. Aravkin, P. Zheng, C. Abbafati, K. M. Abbas, M. Abbasi-Kangevari, F. Abd-Allah, A. Abdelalim, M. Abdollahi, and I. Abdollahpour. 2020. "Global Burden of 87 Risk Factors in 204 Countries and Territories, 1990–2019: A Systematic Analysis for the Global Burden of Disease Study 2019." *Lancet* 396 (10258): 1223–49.

Sánchez-Triana, Ernesto, Santiago Enriquez, Bjorn Larsen, Peter Webster, and Javaid Afzal. 2015. *Sustainability and Poverty Alleviation: Confronting Environmental Threats in Sindh, Pakistan.* Directions in Development—Environment and Sustainable Development;. Washington, DC: World Bank. https://openknowledge.worldbank.org/handle/10986/22149.

UNICEF/Pure Earth. 2020. *The Toxic Truth: Children's Exposure to Lead Pollution Undermines a Generation of Future Potential.* https://www.unicef.org/media/109361/file/The%20toxic %20truth.pdf.

2 Overview: Used Lead-Acid Battery Recycling

This chapter provides an overview of the used lead-acid battery (ULAB) recycling process, including a description of the primary contaminants released or discharged during each step of the process. This chapter also presents a general conceptual site model (CSM) for ULAB sites that identifies the transport mechanisms, exposure pathways, and routes of exposure for local populations that may be exposed to these contaminants. Problem formulation is the process of establishing study objectives, supporting the identification of data-quality objectives associated with statistical analyses, and developing a strategy for characterizing the zone of influence or community footprint associated with ULAB activities in a specific geographic area. A detailed checklist is provided to assist in developing a land-use map of the area and to refine the general CSM for the site of interest based on site-specific existing information and knowledge. The provided checklists highlight key site-specific questions or issues required to inform the selection of participating households and sampling locations at ULAB and associated reference sites.

DESCRIPTION OF THE PROCESS

Used lead-acid battery (ULAB) recycling consists of dismantling and recycling used batteries, usually acquired from motor vehicles. Figure 2.1 provides an overview of the steps involved in the process:

- Collection and transportation of used batteries to a recycling facility
- Dismantling of used batteries
- Separation of component battery parts in a water bath (lead sinks to the bottom and plastics rise to the top)
- Air drying of lead and lead oxide-containing materials; mixing material with coal, soda ash, and scrap metal
- transferring material to uncovered vessels for heating
- Smelting and refining of lead components
- Washing and shredding or melting of plastic components

FIGURE 2.1
Schematic of ULAB activities

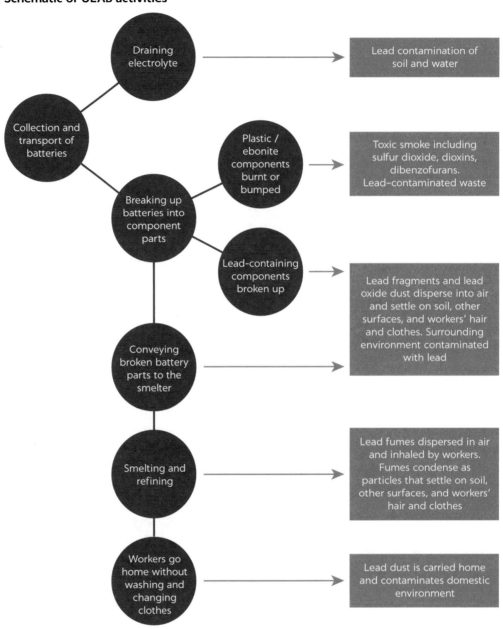

Source: WHO 2017.

- Purification and treatment of sulfuric acid electrolyte (fluid from the batteries)
- Treatment and disposal of waste products (for example, plastics, residual lead, water).

Contaminants and other materials encountered during the ULAB-recycling process arise primarily from the battery components themselves, although some additional materials are added during the smelting and refining process. The primary inputs to the process are summarized in table 2.1.

Contaminants, primarily metals, may enter the environment during various phases of the ULAB-recycling process. Appendix 1 provides a brief overview of the contaminants (metals) typically found at ULAB sites. The primary outputs

TABLE 2.1 **Primary inputs to ULAB-recycling process**

INPUTS	SOURCE
Lead (Pb), arsenic (As), and cadmium (Cd)	Components of battery
Water	Added to separate battery components
Lead oxide, battery acid, and plastics	Components of battery
Coal, soda ash, and scrap metal	Added during smelting and refining

Source: World Bank compilation.

TABLE 2.2 **Primary outputs from the ULAB-recycling process**

OUTPUTS	MECHANISM
Lead (Pb), arsenic (As), and cadmium (Cd)	Released to soil after dismantling batteries
Pb vapor and particulate (including fly ash)	Released to air and soil after smelting
Solid waste containing Pb, As, and Cd	Discharged to unlined lagoons or pits
Wastewater containing Pb, As, and Cd	Discharged to soil or surface water

Source: World Bank compilation.

and contaminants of concern (CoCs) generated as part of the ULAB-recycling process that will be the focus of these guidelines given the stated research objectives are shown in table 2.2.

Once released or discharged into the environment, the contaminants from ULAB-recycling sites can migrate through different environmental media based on their chemical and physical properties and local conditions. The primary transport mechanisms at ULAB-recycling sites include the following:

- Airborne transport of fugitive dust from contaminated surface soil
- Airborne transport of vapors and particulate downwind from the source
- Leaching or runoff of contaminated soil to surface water or groundwater (particularly following rain or flooding events)
- Leaching of waste products from lagoons or pits to surface water or groundwater sources
- Migration of contaminated surface water from wastewater discharges to other surface water sources or groundwater.

CONCEPTUAL SITE MODEL (CSM) OF EXPOSURE

Once contaminants have migrated offsite at ULAB-recycling sites, additional processes or activities can lead to population exposures to these contaminants through direct or indirect contact with contaminated environmental media. For example, populations may be indirectly exposed to contaminants that are present in contaminated water used to irrigate crops or that are present in contaminated soils where livestock are grazed. An *exposure pathway* refers to the physical movement of an agent from a source or point of release through the environment to a receptor (for example, air, groundwater, surface water, soil, sediment, dust, food chain). *Exposure routes* describe the different ways by which agents may enter the body following external contact (for example, inhalation, ingestion, dermal). Potential exposure pathways and routes of exposure related to ULAB-recycling sites are presented in table 2.3.

Figure 2.2 provides a general conceptual site model (CSM) for ULAB-recycling sites that shows how contaminants that are released, emitted, or

TABLE 2.3 **Potential exposure pathways by exposure route and environmental media at ULAB-recycling sites**

EXPOSURE ROUTE	ENVIRONMENTAL MEDIA		
	AIR	SOIL/DUST	WATER
Inhalation	Inhalation of Pb vapors and particles in outdoor air due to releases to air from smelting	Inhalation of Pb soil vapors and Pb, As, or Cd particles or dust in outdoor air due to dismantling batteries, releases to soil from smelting, and solid waste or wastewater discharges to soil	Inhalation of Pb vapors released from tap, surface, or groundwater (for example, bathing, showering, washing, swimming) due to solid waste or wastewater discharges to water
	Inhalation of Pb vapors and particles in indoor air due to releases to air from smelting	Inhalation of Pb soil vapors and Pb, As, or Cd particles or dust in indoor air due to dismantling batteries, releases to soil from smelting, and solid waste or wastewater discharges to soil	
Ingestion	Ingestion of agricultural products contaminated with Pb, As, or Cd due to deposition of vapors or particles (for example, fruits, vegetables, grains)	Incidental ingestion of Pb, As, or Cd in soil or dust (indoors or outdoors) due to dismantling batteries, releases to soil from smelting, and solid waste or wastewater discharges to soil	Ingestion of Pb, As, or Cd in tap, surface, or groundwater due to solid waste or wastewater discharges to water
	Ingestion of agricultural products contaminated with Pb, As, or Cd due to transfer of contaminants from air to animals or plants to animals (for example, meat, milk, eggs)	Ingestion of agricultural products contaminated with Pb, As, or Cd due to transfer of contaminants from soil to plants, animals, or plants to animals	Ingestion of agricultural products contaminated with Pb, As, or Cd due to being irrigated with contaminated water
			Ingestion of agricultural products contaminated with Pb, As, or Cd due to transfer of contaminants from water to animals
Dermal contact	Dermal contact with Pb vapors and particles due to releases to air from smelting	Dermal contact with Pb, As, or Cd in soil or dust (indoors or outdoors) due to dismantling batteries, releases to soil from smelting, and solid waste or wastewater discharges to soil	Dermal contact with Pb, As, or Cd in tap, surface, or groundwater due to solid waste or wastewater discharges to water

Source: World Bank compilation.
Note: As = arsenic; Cd = cadmium; Pb = lead.

FIGURE 2.2
General conceptual site model for ULAB recycling

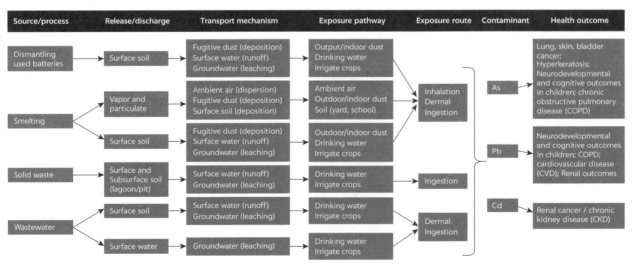

Source: von Stackelberg, Williams, and Sánchez-Triana 2021.

discharged from ULAB sources can migrate through the environment, and the pathways and routes by which individuals in the population can be exposed to those contaminants. Per the *General Guidelines for Environmental Sampling* (chapter 4), samples should be collected from different environmental media at each ULAB-recycling site to provide data on exposure point concentrations for a subset of the most relevant contaminants, exposure pathways, and populations of interest. Appendix C provides links to key references and resource guides to facilitate environmental field sampling and sample laboratory analysis.

LINKING ENVIRONMENTAL CONTAMINATION TO HUMAN EXPOSURES AND HEALTH OUTCOMES

Exposure is the amount of an agent in the environmental media with which a person comes into contact and is a function of the exposure point concentration and the amount of time the individual is in contact with the contaminated media. *Intake* is the amount of an agent that enters the human body via an exposure route. Characterizing exposure and intake therefore requires information about various *exposure factors*—such as human behavior, time, and activity patterns— and contact rates. Common exposure factors relevant for ULAB-recycling sites include the following:

- Soil and dust ingestion rates
- Water-ingestion rates and liquid-ingestion rates
- Food-ingestion rates and fish-ingestion rates
- Inhalation rates
- Mouthing frequency in children (hand-to-mouth and object-to-mouth)
- Dermal exposure factors (for example, skin-surface area, skin adherence, residue transfer)
- Time spent indoors vs. outdoors
- Time spent in various activities (for example, sleeping, at school, at work)
- Time spent bathing, showering, or swimming
- Time spent playing on various surfaces (for example, dirt, grass, sand, gravel)
- Body weight.

Although information on typical or recommended exposure factors is often available for high-income countries (HICs), these data may not be reliable or accurate for assessing exposures in LMICs. Per the *General Guidelines for Conducting Household Surveys* (appendix B), site- and population-specific information should be collected to provide relevant exposure-factors data for use at ULAB-recycling sites and associated reference sites. This information will be linked to the environmental sampling data (obtained from chapter 4) as one way to estimate population-level exposures at ULAB-recycling sites as compared to reference sites.

Dose is the amount of an agent that crosses the outer boundary of an organism and is absorbed into the body and thus is available for interaction with metabolic processes. The internal dose of a chemical (or its metabolite) can be measured directly from biological sampling (often called biomonitoring). Depending on the contaminant, common biological matrices that may be relevant for ULAB-recycling sites include the following:

- Blood
- Urine

TABLE 2.4 **Health outcomes associated with CoCs at ULAB-recycling sites**

METALS	MEASURABLE HEALTH OUTCOMES
Pb	Developmental health outcomes in children (for example, reduction in IQ, cognitive deficits)
	Cardiovascular-health outcomes in adults
	Renal-health outcomes in children and adults
As	Skin rashes and lesions and hyperkeratosis, possible precursors to skin cancer
	Developmental and cognitive deficits in children
	Lung cancer in adults
	Bladder cancer in adults
Cd	Nephrotoxicity and renal effects, possible precursors to kidney cancer

Source: World Bank compilation.

- Hair
- Nails (that is, toenails, fingernails)
- Breast milk / cord blood.

Per the *General Guidelines for Biological Sampling* (chapter 5), samples should be collected from relevant biological matrices, where feasible, at each ULAB site to provide data on total exposures from all sources and pathways (as reflected by the measured internal dose). This information will be linked to the household-survey data (chapter 3) and exposure concentration (chapter 4) to assess the relationship between estimates of exposure and biomarkers of exposure. Appendix D provides links to key resources and methods for collecting biological samples. Where possible, these data can be used to validate or update existing modeling tools (appendix D) for estimating population exposures and doses. Note that prior to collecting any biological samples, the in-field team will need to ensure that all Institutional Review Board (IRB), human subjects, and ethical clearances are completed as required. Population exposures to the predominant contaminants at ULAB-recycling sites may be associated with different types of health outcomes, as shown in table 2.4.

Per the *General Guidelines for Assessing Medical and Health Outcomes* (chapter 6), medical exams, surveys, and diagnostic testing should be conducted, where feasible and appropriate, at each small-scale ULAB site and associated reference site to provide data on reported, observed, or measured symptoms and health effects. This information will be linked to the household survey (chapter 3), environmental concentrations (chapter 4), and biological dose measurements (chapter 5) to assess the potential relationship between exposures and health outcomes at these ULAB sites as compared to reference sites. Appendix E provides links to key tools and resources for assessing health outcomes.

Figure 2.3 provides an overview of how the data collected at each ULAB-recycling site will be used to link environmental contamination to human exposures and health outcomes.

Problem formulation and site-specific characterization

Problem formulation is the process of establishing study objectives, supporting the identification of data-quality objectives associated with statistical analyses, and developing a strategy for characterizing the zone of influence or community footprint associated with ULAB activities in a specific geographic area. A key

FIGURE 2.3

Overview of how site data will be used to link environmental contamination to human exposures and health outcomes

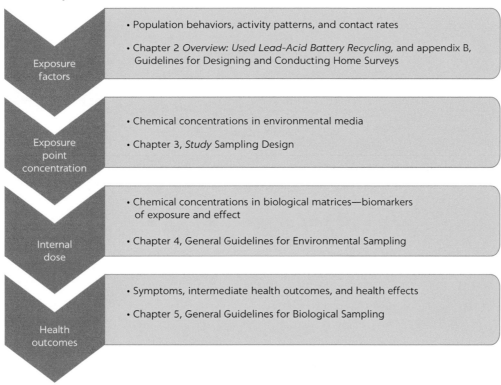

Source: World Bank compilation.

first step is to develop a land-use map of the area and refine the general CSM for the site of interest based on site-specific existing information and knowledge. This will set the stage for subsequent collection of environmental, household survey, biomonitoring, and health-outcomes data given the goal of relating measured environmental exposures to biomonitoring and health-outcome data at the individual level.

The primary objective of these guidelines is to guide research to assess the relationship between environmental contamination, exposures, and health outcomes related to a subset of contaminants originating from ULAB activities (for example, lead [Pb], arsenic [As], and cadmium [Cd]) for particularly vulnerable populations (for example, children and women of child-bearing age) within a single household at ULAB-recycling sites in LMICs. To evaluate this objective, biomonitoring, health-outcome, and household-survey data are linked to environmental data (for example, soil, dust, water, agricultural products) for individuals comprising an "exposed" population compared to individuals comprising an "unexposed" population. Statistical analyses of the data obtained during this research can help answer questions such as the following:

- What are the environmental concentrations of Pb, As, and Cd in the vicinity of ULAB facilities? Are these higher than in comparable areas without such facilities?
- What are the biological concentrations of Pb, As, and Cd in blood, hair, or urine? Do these levels correlate with environmental concentrations? Do they

differ between ULAB-exposed populations and non–ULAB-exposed populations?

- What is the incidence of specific health outcomes in ULAB-exposed populations? Do these correlate with environmental or biological concentrations? Do they differ from non–ULAB-exposed populations?
- How do time-activity patterns and exposure factors differ across populations? Do these differences help explain the biological or health-outcome findings?
- Which data sets are most predictive of exposures or health outcomes? Is there a reduced set of data that can be collected in the future to streamline the evaluation of potential impacts from ULAB activities?
- Can an assessment framework be developed to evaluate the benefits and costs of potential interventions to reduce exposures or improve population health?

The problem-formulation stage defines the questions that the analysis will address. A goal of problem formulation is to assemble existing site information and data to inform an understanding of how ULAB-recycling activities might affect the local population. Such data regarding sites and effects are used to develop a land-use map of the area. The map may be developed using local topographical maps, Google Maps, Google Earth, GIS programs, or similar software. The map should include a defined geographic area (for example, village, town, city) that locates the physical small-scale ULAB facility or processing area (that is, "source area") relative to other infrastructure or areas where populations, particularly children, spend the most time (for example, housing units, schools, town center, and so forth) since these define the potential zone of influence or footprint associated with ULAB activities. For the purposes of these guidelines, these areas are collectively referred to as the "ULAB study site" (see box 2.1) and include both the source area and the broader zone of influence. Additional maps or insets provide the spatial context for activities that may lead to contaminant exposures. For example, within the source area, the map should identify processing activities and physical waste stored onsite (for example, slag, matte, fly-ash lagoons, waste pits). The map should also identify the prevailing wind direction and the location of local wells or water bodies (particularly those used as drinking-water sources or for recreational purposes) as well as direct and indirect wastewater discharges (including proximity to freshwater and sources of drinking water). The site map will also serve as the basis for

BOX 2.1

Hypothetical ULAB-recycling facility

Consider a hypothetical ULAB-recycling facility located in a town setting (population 12,000) with some residences located within 100 m of the source. Land use at the site is primarily residential, agricultural, and light industrial. There are three schools at the site. The source area experiences frequent rain and runoff into the nearby residential area, as well as truck traffic along the road leading into the facility. A number of creeks and ditches are found at the site, and

most households obtain drinking water from private or shared wells, while the remaining households obtain their water from a shared surface-water source. Nearly half the residents have backyard gardens, and the rest obtain much of their produce and meat from a local market. There is a large-scale agricultural field near the ULAB-recycling facility. There are also uninhabited areas that have a low potential for exposures to occur.

identifying relevant environmental sampling locations (chapter 4) as well as households from which to collect home survey data (chapter 3 and appendix B), biomonitoring data (chapter 5), and health-outcome data (chapter 6).

Another goal of problem formulation is to refine the general CSM for ULAB sites to reflect any unique characteristics of the study area, identify the site-specific relevant exposure pathways and exposed populations of interest. Thus, problem formulation is used to characterize all aspects of the environmental setting and determine where and under what conditions general population exposures are likeliest to occur. The following checklist is designed as a guide to assist in characterizing and mapping the environmental setting and establishing the zone of influence to develop the site-specific CSM.

Characterize the general environmental setting on a map:

- Locate ULAB activities in the context of local populations, noting where different aspects of the process may occur. In some areas, battery breaking may occur in areas separate from the primary smelting and refining.
- Identify locations of all surface waters, including ditches, creeks, streams, rivers, and lakes.
- Identify what is known about groundwater, depth to the water table, and aquifers in the study area.
- Identify the prevailing wind direction, particularly relative to residential areas, local bodies of water, and small- or large-scale agricultural activities. Dispersion and deposition of lead dust and other metals are likely to be significant and can occur over large areas.
- Identify water bodies within a depositional area of ULAB activities, or affected by wastewaters or soil runoff, both of which are likely to contain lead and other metals.
- Identify agricultural areas, community gardens, and the potential for backyard gardening.
- Locate sources of irrigation water that might be affected by ULAB wastewater discharges, including direct or indirect surface-water discharges or releases to soils that can run off or erode. Establish whether groundwater is used for irrigation and whether there is a leaching pathway.
- Identify locations where animals or animal products (for example, milk, eggs) are raised for consumption.

Describe the ULAB process:

- Identify how many batteries are being processed, and whether other lead-containing items are also recycled (for example, metal parts).
- Identify where batteries are stored and what happens to the plastic casings once battery breaking is completed. In some communities, these plastic casings are repurposed in homes in different ways and may become a source of exposures.
- Battery dismantling typically involves a water bath to separate the plastic from the lead—where does this water come from and how does disposal occur?
- Describe how smelting occurs (for example, blast furnace, open barrels, other vessels). Identify the number and capacity of smelting vessels.
- Describe the refining process, including identifying the number and capacity of refining vessels.
- Describe any measures for air-pollution control utilized during smelting and refining.

- Identify what is done with any waste products from the stack (for example, dust from filters on any equipment for air-pollution control).
- Describe the specific ULAB process utilized and identify all inputs and outputs (for example, the processes identified in figure 2.1).
- Identify how much slag is produced for each ton of metallic lead. Typically, 300–350 kg of slag is produced per ton of metallic lead, and approximately 5 percent of this slag is composed of lead compounds. Generally, slag is recycled until there is no viable metal left to be extracted; at that point, the slag is typically disposed of in specific designated areas. Locate these areas and describe the conditions of storage and opportunities for material to enter the environment (for example, runoff from routine precipitation events, flooding, and so on).
- Identify the disposition of leachate that may be produced; unstable, water-soluble slag that comes into contact with water or moist air is likely to lead to downstream contamination.
- Describe the process for handling the electrolyte solution. This solution will contain high levels of sulfuric acid that require neutralization.
- Cooling water is often used and, although it typically does not come into contact with contaminants, there may be aspects to the site-specific process in which this is not true and must be identified.

Waste releases and potential fate and transport:

- Develop a qualitative (or quantitative, if possible) mass balance for ULAB activities by identifying all materials used in the process, where they come from, and what products, including waste, are generated.
- Locate wastewater discharges on the site map and identify the specific hydrologic connections between wastewater discharges and surface waters (for example, ditches, lagoons, receiving waters).
- Establish whether typical precipitation events lead to routine ponding and discharges to nearby surface waters.
- Locate communal surface or groundwater sources of drinking water relative to potentially affected surface waters on the site map to identify potential sampling areas.
- Establish the potential for wastewater discharges (directly or indirectly through surface water) to be used as irrigation water for local agricultural products or animals.
- In some areas, the plastic from battery breaking.

Population demographics and exposure pathways:

- Establish the local population and population size (for example, village, urban, peri-urban).
- Quantify or estimate population size and age/sex distribution.
- Identify the fraction of the local population that participates in ULAB activities.
- Identify residential areas relative to ULAB activities on the site map.
- Identify and map community spaces within the study area, including schools, hospitals and health centers, community centers, places of worship, playgrounds, and places where individuals, particularly children, are likely to spend significant amounts of time.
- If processing activities occur in homes (for example, grinding and milling), these specific locations should be explicitly identified.

- Establish site-specific exposure pathways (as shown in figure 2.2).
- Identify whether unique or additional exposure pathways should be considered. Particular emphasis should be given to identifying the sources of drinking water, since Pb in drinking water can represent a significant exposure pathway at lead-contaminated sites.

The general guidelines provided in the following chapters should be used to support data-collection efforts at each ULAB-recycling site. These guidelines provide a general (uniform) approach for sampling and analysis, but detailed field protocols (for example, physical process of collecting samples, storing and shipping samples, laboratory analysis of samples) and sampling data sheets will need to be provided by the in-field research team, recognizing that local analytical capacity to implement these guidelines will differ across countries. Local implementation may involve an iterative process, in which initially split samples are collected and sent for analysis locally as well as to an accredited international laboratory for a standard interlaboratory comparison. Enhancing and leveraging local capacity to conduct sampling, analyze samples, and interpret results is expected to require flexibility and collaboration.

REFERENCES

von Stackelberg, Katherine, Pamela R. D. Williams, and Ernesto Sánchez-Triana. 2021. "A Systematic Framework for Collecting Site-Specific Sampling and Survey Data to Support Analyses of Health Impacts from Land-Based Pollution in Low- and Middle-Income Countries." *Int. J. Environ. Res. Public Health* 18: 4676. https://doi.org/10.3390/ijerph18094676.

WHO (World Health Organization). 2017. *Recycling Used Lead-Acid Batteries: Health Considerations*. Geneva: WHO.

3 Study Sampling Design

This chapter describes the process for identifying participating households and individuals within those households that will provide household-survey data (appendix B), environmental sampling data (chapter 4), biomonitoring data (chapter 5), and health-outcomes data (chapter 6). Identifying participating households is a critical step that will determine where to conduct subsequent environmental sampling of soil, sediment, dust, water, fish, or agricultural and food products, and for whom to collect biological and health-outcome data for assessing the potential contribution of used lead-acid battery (ULAB)–related contamination to population-level exposures and health outcomes in exposed individuals.

To meet the primary research objective, the sampling design is structured to link environmental contamination and individual exposures to multiple contaminants of concern (CoCs), with different health outcomes associated with exposure to these CoCs at the household level. Selected households and sampling locations should therefore provide data on how environmental contamination contributes to household exposures, rather than identifying local hot spots or fully characterizing environmental concentrations across the entire site, which will likely require a different sampling strategy. These guidelines recommend a primary grid-based sampling-design strategy augmented by targeted sampling on where individuals spend significant amounts of time (for example, schools, playgrounds, agricultural locations, recreational or commercial fishing areas). Targeted sampling will be required for households associated with fish consumption from potentially affected aquatic areas. Typical grid densities range from 20 x 20 m to 100 x 100 m, with most falling generally in the 40 x 40 m to 60 x 60 m range. A household is selected from each grid node with an example provided.

Recommendations for the home-survey questionnaire are designed to provide the detailed information on exposure factors such as time-activity patterns, food-frequency questionnaires, and other demographic information used to link environmental sampling data with biomonitoring data and health-outcome data in a specific community. As these data are collected, they should be compiled into country- or region-specific databases to support development of risk assessments and other analyses that require quantifying exposure factors (for example, consumption rates, body weight, and so forth) to predict, for example, contaminant-specific intake rates applicable to analyses beyond ULAB sites.

INTRODUCTION

To meet the primary objective outlined above, the sampling design is structured to link environmental contamination and individual exposures to multiple CoCs with different health outcomes associated with these CoCs at the household level. Selected households and sampling locations should therefore provide data on how environmental contamination contributes to household exposures, rather than identifying local hot spots or fully characterizing environmental concentrations across the entire site. For purposes of these guidelines, individuals selected within each household should also reflect those populations of greatest vulnerability, such as children and women of childbearing age. As noted in chapter 2, the primary CoCs at ULAB-recycling sites are lead (Pb), arsenic (As), and cadmium (Cd). These metals will persist in the environment in their original form and are likely to be found in soil, dust, water, and some agricultural products. Determining where to collect environmental samples (that is, households and other targeted locations) at each ULAB-recycling site should be informed by knowledge of the source location, contaminant release and transport mechanisms, likely exposure pathways, and location and activities of populations exposed, per the refined conceptual site model (CSM) and household survey discussed in chapter 2.

IDENTIFYING HOUSEHOLDS AND SAMPLING LOCATIONS

Identifying the households and other targeted sampling locations linked to where individuals spend time at each ULAB-recycling site is a critical first step prior to any in-field data-collection efforts.

In these guidelines, a predominantly grid-based sampling design is recommended for identifying participating households, which helps ensure randomization in the selection process, followed by targeted sampling as appropriate. In grid-based sampling, households are identified using regularly spaced intervals defined by a grid placed over the study area. Within each household, children 10 years of age and younger represent the primary population of interest for these guidelines, given that (a) Pb is the primary CoC at ULAB-recycling sites, (b) children have a greater opportunity for Pb exposures due to age-specific activity patterns and on a per body weight basis, and (c) tools are available for evaluating specific health outcomes (for example, cognitive deficits) associated with elevated childhood Pb exposures. However, to maximize the participation rate (in the event that sampling children only is a deterrent for some households), both the youngest child (3 years or older) and his or her mother should be targeted for data collection once specific households have been identified.

Although a more refined approach for selecting households at each site can be tailored by the in-field research team once the specific ULAB-recycling sites have been identified, the following steps will aid in identifying households and environmental sampling locations at these sites using a consistent and uniform approach:

- *Step 1.* Based on the site map developed in chapter 2, overlay an equally spaced grid (typically a square or rectangle, but this can be a circle or other shape) on the site map with the source area at the center, assuming the source area is surrounded by residential areas. Depending on the site, the source area may not be centered within a residential area and the grid will need to be adjusted accordingly to capture locations designed to maximize potential exposures. The goal is to identify households within the zone of influence of the source area, as informed by the site-specific CSM (chapter 2). Determining the exact grid size (which affects sample size) will require some flexibility, depending on the site-specific CSM, population density, and resource constraints. For example, at a site with known wastewater discharges to a stream that flows several kilometers downstream from the source area, ultimately discharging to a pond, it may be beneficial to select both households within 1 km of the source area as well as other households from downstream locations. In general, the literature suggests that the majority of the influence of ULAB facilities on soil and dust contamination occurs within several km of the source and drops off after 1 km (see the bibliography in appendix F) but will vary depending on site-specific attributes of the exposed population. Typical grid densities range from 20 x 20 m to 100 x 100 m, with most falling generally in the 40 x 40 m to 60 x 60 m range. A household is selected from each grid node. If a selected household is not willing to participate in the study, a neighboring household in the same grid space should be chosen. The sample size can be altered by choice of grid size—that is, reducing the grid size will increase the number of sample nodes and households sampled, while increasing the grid size will reduce the number of sample nodes and households sampled. Although it is not possible to identify a predetermined sample size for each site using power calculations, in order to balance research objectives and feasibility constraints, it is recommended that more than 100 households, but fewer than 400 households, be selected per ULAB-recycling site (average of 200 to 300 households).[1] See appendix B for additional references.

- *Step 2.* For all households identified in Step 1, select two household members to participate in the study. All subsequent environmental, biological, and health-outcome sampling will link back to the specific characteristics and activity patterns of these individuals, which will be informed by the home-survey responses. As noted above, the primary population of interest for this study is children ages 10 or younger, and one child and the child's mother should be selected. However, some households may not contain children within this age grouping or provide permission for a young child to participate in the study. In these situations, an older child under the age of 18 and the child's mother should be selected, if possible; otherwise, seek permission for any adult in the household.

  As an example of how individual households might be selected, consider the hypothetical ULAB-recycling facility mentioned earlier, which is (hypothetically) centrally located within a residential area of approximately 800 x 1,100 m = 880,000 m². A grid size of 50 x 50 m = 2,500 m² placed over this area yields 352 grid nodes (880,000 ÷ 2,500), but a number of these grid nodes do not contain any nearby households. Subtracting these uninhabited areas from the total results in 170 grid nodes, from which 170 households are selected for inclusion in the study.

- *Step 3.* Individuals who agree to provide survey, biomonitoring, and health-outcome data may not spend all of their time at home, particularly children, who are likely to attend school. Given the objective to link the home survey, biomonitoring, and health-outcome data to environmental exposures, the home survey should be conducted as soon as the households and participating individuals have been identified. Information gathered from the survey will provide important data on additional targeted sampling locations (for example, schools, playgrounds, community centers, and other areas where participating individuals spend time), as well as communal drinking-water sources and specific agricultural products being consumed. Appendix B provides sample questions and additional information on designing household questionnaires.

The home-survey questionnaire (summarized in table 2.1 and described more fully in appendix B) provides the detailed information on such exposure factors as time-activity patterns, food-frequency questionnaires, and other demographic information used to link environmental sampling data (chapter 4) with biomonitoring data (chapter 5) and health-outcome data (chapter 6) in a specific community. However, as these kinds of data are collected, this information should be compiled into country- or region-specific databases to support development of risk assessments and other analyses that require quantifying exposure factors (for example, consumption rates, body weight, and so forth) to predict, for example, contaminant-specific intake rates. Standardized tables of exposure factors (for example, the US EPA Exposure Factors Handbook [US EPA 2011]) have been derived for specific countries, but it is not clear how these data represent communities from areas with different cultural and lifestyle attributes.

In general, each participating individual (and/or a parent on behalf of a child) will answer the types of questions shown in table 3.1.

- *Step 4.* For each ULAB-recycling site, identify a matched reference site that has similar features and population characteristics (but which does not participate in ULAB recycling and is expected to experience similar

TABLE 3.1 **Categories of questions in the home survey (appendix B)**

CATEGORY	TYPE OF QUESTIONS
General demographics	Age, sex, length of residence, education, income, household size and composition
Occupation and school	Work and school activities, possibility for take-home / exposures outside of the home
Time-activity patterns and lifestyle	Exposure factors and lifestyle and housing details, including other possible sources of exposure
Dietary information	Calculate intake rates based on a food-frequency questionnaire (FFQ), with an emphasis on information about consumption of locally produced agricultural products (either home garden or purchased). FFQs can be done by keeping a diary over some time period or recall over some time period (for example, 24-hour recall). Can be combined with a duplicate diet analysis. Also note drinking-water sources (communal untreated, municipal treated) and amount of water and water-based beverage consumption
Economic data	Cost-of-illness
Health status	Self-reported symptoms: may be superseded by an on-site or off-site medical examination in conjunction with biomonitoring (chapter 5) and health-outcome evaluation and testing (chapter 6)

Source: World Bank compilation.

environmental exposures in the absence of ULAB activities) and conduct sampling at this site in the same manner as at the ULAB-recycling site. This step is recommended, given the objective to determine the association between site-related contamination and health outcomes in the general population. The statistical comparison between two populations similar in every way except for the exposure of interest (for example, no ULAB activities of any kind in the reference population) will provide important insights into site-related contamination. It is possible to evaluate associations without a reference population, but the results may not be as definitive.

Note that achieving an objective other than the primary objective identified here might require a different sampling approach or different sample-size requirements. For example, a fuller characterization of environmental CoC concentrations throughout a study area without also collecting biomonitoring and health-outcome data might require additional environmental sampling (for example, soil, dust, or water) than is recommended in chapter 4, which targets individual households and other locations where individuals spend the most time in order to link environmental exposures most efficiently and effectively with biomonitoring and health-outcome data. Similarly, a study focused on characterizing population exposures to CoCs based on biomonitoring data (chapter 5) in the absence of environmental data may require a larger grid over a larger area to ensure a representative sample of the general population.

NOTE

1. Note that because the current study design is focused on multiple CoCs and exploratory associations between multiple endpoints (for example, environmental contamination, individual exposures, several possible health outcomes per CoC), it is not possible to conduct a single statistical power calculation to determine optimal sample size at ULAB-recycling sites. A useful reference is the WHO publication by Lwanga and Lemeshow (1991), titled *Sample Size Determination in Health Studies: A Practical Manual*, which provides tables of minimum numbers of samples given specific hypotheses and inputs. In general, power calculations involving contaminant exposures and health outcomes will depend on the statistical approach(es) to be used in analyzing the data, anticipated effect sizes, or the difference between two populations. Additionally, these calculations will be based on (a) anticipated probability of a health outcome given no exposure (general prevalence in the population), (b) anticipated relative risk, (c) confidence level, (d) significance level, and (e) relative precision.

REFERENCES

Lwanga, Stephen Kaggwa, Stanley Lemeshow, and World Health Organization. 1991. *Sample Size Determination in Health Studies: A Practical Manual*. Geneva: World Health Organization. https://apps.who.int/iris/handle/10665/40062.

US EPA (US Environmental Protection Agency). 2011. *Exposure Factors Handbook 2011 Edition* (Final Report); EPA/600/R-09/052F. US EPA Office for Research and Development. Washington, DC: US EPA.

4 General Guidelines for Environmental Sampling

This chapter provides an overview of environmental media that may be affected by used lead-acid battery (ULAB) activities, as well as specific recommendations for sampling strategies at each household and sampling area. It also makes recommendations for appropriate analytical methodologies, and it provides a running example for identifying sampling locations and collecting and analyzing samples from each participating household and targeted sampling area.

INTRODUCTION

Environmental samples will be used to determine the overall magnitude of contamination at each ULAB-recycling site, with an emphasis on those areas where populations of interest (for example, children) spend the most time. This chapter provides general guidelines for identifying where to collect environmental samples at each site (sampling design) and what types of samples should be collected from different environmental media. Important factors that will need to be considered on a site-by-site basis are also noted. Detailed protocols and procedures for collecting a physical sample, handling and preparing a physical sample, and laboratory analysis of a physical samples are not addressed here and will be developed by the in-field research team based on existing guidance, as summarized in appendix C. It is essential that the environmental sampling be conducted for the same homes and individuals for whom the home survey (appendix C), biomonitoring (chapter 5), and health-outcome (chapter 6) data are collected. The same type of environmental samples should also be collected from both the identified ULAB-recycling sites and matched reference sites. Note that any necessary ethical clearances will need to be obtained prior to sample collection by the in-field research team.

The in-field research team should provide detailed protocols and procedures for collecting a physical sample, handling and preparing physical samples, and laboratory analysis of physical samples. Field observation and data sheets should also be provided by the in-field research team. It is important that all sampling tools and containers be clean and free of contaminants prior to sampling.

SOIL SAMPLING

Exposure pathways and routes

The primary contaminants of concern (CoCs) released or discharged at ULAB-recycling sites into the environment are lead (Pb), arsenic (As), and cadmium (Cd). Because these metals do not degrade easily in the environment, they are likely to be found in both surface and subsurface soils at ULAB-recycling sites. Populations in contact with soil, particularly surface soil, at ULAB-recycling sites include both adults and children, although the latter are more likely to have direct and more frequent contact with surface soil because of their behaviors and activity patterns. Dermal contact and incidental, direct, and indirect ingestion of contaminated surface soils are the primary routes and pathways of exposure at ULAB-recycling sites. Dermal exposures can occur when adults or children walk barefoot on surface soil or their body touches this soil (for example, during play outdoors). Incidental ingestion can occur when individuals get soil on their skin (for example, fingers) or an object (for example, a toy), which then comes into contact with their mouth or food. Direct ingestion can occur when individuals eat dirt or soil (this is a common practice among some children and generally still involves the top layer of soil), whereas indirect ingestion can occur when crops (for example, below-ground root vegetables) are grown in contaminated soil or are affected by fugitive dust or airborne soils (for example, above-ground leafy vegetables). The agricultural sampling exposure pathway is discussed below.

Sampling protocol and analysis

Soil samples should be collected at each ULAB-recycling site (and reference site) using the grid-sampling approach described above. Specifically, soil samples should be collected near the ULAB source area and in areas corresponding to selected households (for example, yard, garden). Additional targeted soil samples should be collected at schools or daycare facilities (for example, playground) or from any other outdoor area where participating household members spend significant amounts of time (for example, outdoor recreational areas). It is important that specific sampling locations within each grid or targeted location be optimized relative to where individuals spend the most time (for example, a child playing in a yard versus near the front door, a child playing in a playground at school versus in a parking lot). Determining where to collect these samples should be informed by the refined conceptual site model (CSM) and household survey (chapter 2). Note that sample locations should preferably consist of bare soil that is not covered with grass, vegetation, or other material. Because individuals are more likely to come into contact with surface soils than subsurface soils, only surface-soil sampling is recommended at ULAB-recycling sites.

When collecting soil samples, the following general guidelines should be followed (see box 4.1):

- Identify four individual undisturbed (or minimally disturbed) soil-sampling locations per grid node or targeted location. The four locations should be representative of the entire area(s) where the population of interest spends the most time and over which activities occur. This could involve collecting the four samples from different spots at the same location (for example, front yard or garden) or from different spots at multiple locations (for example, front yard and backyard).

BOX 4.1

Soil sampling at a hypothetical ULAB-recycling site

A total of 170 households and three schools were selected under the grid-based and targeted sampling design. Since this site is located in a more rural setting, children spend the bulk of their time at home or at school, rather than central playgrounds or other outdoor settings. Consequently, soil sampling is only conducted at the identified households and schools, resulting in a total of 173 composite soil samples collected at this site. Each composite sample comprises four individual samples per location, which are analyzed for Pb, As, and Cd in the field using an XRF analyzer. The composite samples are packaged and sent to an accredited laboratory for analysis of Pb, As, and Cd at a minimum and possibly additional bioavailability analysis of Pb and As.

Soil sampling at homes or schools includes those areas where individuals spend the most time (for example, front yard or back yard, garden, playground). The emphasis is on those individuals for whom the home survey, biological sampling, and health-outcome data will be collected, and these individuals also represent the focal point for all environmental sampling.

For example, consider the four sampling scenarios in table B4.1.1. **Important note:** *soil sampling should occur in the same households or locations where other environmental samples are being collected and which relate to individuals providing biomonitoring and health-outcome data.*

TABLE B4.1.1 **Soil sampling scenarios**

SCENARIO	INDIVIDUAL	TIME ACTIVITY	SAMPLING LOCATIONS
1	5-year-old child (female) and her 28-year-old mother	Front yard	4 random samples collected from front yard (1 composite)
2	6-year-old child (male) and his 30-year-old mother	Front yard and backyard	2 random samples collected from both front yard and backyard (1 composite)
3	35-year-old woman (no child)	Backyard garden	4 random samples collected from garden (1 composite)
4	10-year-old child (male) (mother is not participating)	School playground	4 random samples collected from play area (1 composite)

Source: World Bank compilation.

- Record all four sampling locations using GPS and document coordinates on the site map.
- Collect the surface-soil samples at a depth of 0 to 10 cm (note: the zero level starts from the surface after removal of any vegetation, fresh litter, and surface stones).
- First, use an in-field X-ray fluorescence (XRF) analyzer to measure the soil Pb, As, and Cd concentration for each of the four individual soil samples per sampling location. Note that the XRF instrument can be simultaneously calibrated for additional metals.
- After XRF analysis, combine the four individual soil samples per sampling location into a single composite soil sample. Package and send this composite sample to an accredited laboratory for analysis using guidelines provided by the laboratory for sample preservation, packaging, and shipping. It is recommended that the composite samples be analyzed using ICP-MS methods, which are considered state-of-the art for metals analysis (appendix C).
- Follow the directions and use the sampling equipment provided or recommended by the in-field research team and analytical laboratory with respect to sample collection, preparation, and shipping (including use of personal protective equipment, such as gloves).

- *Optional:* Due to the specific environmental properties of both Pb and As, the ideal analytical method in soil measures the bioavailable fraction rather than the total fraction of these metals. Bioavailability is important from a risk-assessment perspective since it measures the fraction of an ingested dose that crosses the gastrointestinal epithelium and becomes available for distribution to internal target tissues and organs. Therefore, in addition to the traditional laboratory analysis for all soil samples, it is recommended that half of all household samples (50 percent) and all (100 percent) of targeted samples (for example, schools, playgrounds) be analyzed for bioavailable Pb using EPA Method 1340 (US EPA, n.d.) or similar, if feasible. Note that, at this time, this method has only been validated by the US EPA for Pb, although a method has been proposed for As. The in-field research team will need to determine whether it is feasible to conduct this extra analysis given possible resource constraints. Appendix C provides more information on sampling methods and links to standards and guidelines.

DUST SAMPLING

Exposure pathways and routes

ULAB-recycling sites result in direct releases of vapors and particulate as well indirect releases of fugitive dust from contaminated surface soil. The particulates and fugitive dust may contain Pb, As, and Cd, with which both adults and children may come into contact at ULAB-recycling sites. Dermal contact, incidental ingestion, and inhalation of contaminated dust are the primary exposure routes and pathways at ULAB-recycling sites. Indoor exposures to contaminated dust (the source of which may have been tracked in from outdoors) is of particular concern due to the duration, frequency, and proximity of individuals' contact with indoor surfaces. Dermal exposures can occur when adults or children walk barefoot on dust or when an individual's skin touches the dust (for example, during sleep or play). Incidental ingestion can occur when individuals get dust on their skin (for example, fingers) or an object (for example, a toy), which then comes into contact with their mouth or food. This is a particularly significant exposure pathway for children at ULAB-recycling sites. Inhalation can occur from direct releases of fugitive dust or when settled dust becomes resuspended (for example, sweeping a floor, wiping surfaces). Although it is possible for inhalation exposures to occur, this pathway is likely to be small relative to the other exposure pathways, so air sampling is not recommended here.

Sampling protocol and analysis

Indoor dust samples should be collected at each ULAB-recycling site and reference site for each household where soil samples were collected as well as the targeted locations (for example, schools) where soil samples were collected, if applicable. As was the case for soil sampling, it is important that specific sampling areas within each location be optimized relative to where individuals spend the most time (for example, children's bedroom and living room in homes, classroom or lunchroom at school). Note that outdoor-dust samples are of limited utility given the collection of soil samples and are not recommended here.

Typical dust samples are taken on indoor surfaces such as floors, tables, and windowsills. Specific methods for sampling dust at ULAB-recycling sites will differ depending on the surface substrate. For dwellings with dirt floors, methods analogous to soil sampling should be used. For dwellings with impervious and smooth surfaces (for example, wood floors, wood tables, windowsills), wipe samples are preferred. In some instances, vacuum sampling may be required, such as for carpeted surfaces or rough surfaces—for example, brick, stone, and so forth.

Similar to soil sampling, dust samples should undergo two levels of analysis if possible. First, individual dust samples should be analyzed in the field using an XRF analyzer calibrated for Pb, As, and Cd. The XRF can also be simultaneously calibrated for additional metals. Second, composite dust samples should be packaged and sent to an independent (accredited) laboratory for analysis of Pb, As, and Cd. As noted above, other metals may also be evaluated by the analytical laboratory if a multi-screen metals analysis is requested. The bioavailability method described above for soil sampling is not suitable for dust samples, so it is not recommended here.

When collecting dust samples using the wipe method, the following general guidelines should be followed (see box 4.2):

- Collect two or three individual dust samples within each household or other targeted indoor location. These locations should be representative of the

---

BOX 4.2

Dust sampling at a hypothetical ULAB-recycling site

Indoor dust sampling should be collected from the same households and targeted locations (for example, schools) identified for soil sampling. In this example, this yields sampling at 170 households and 3 schools, for a total of 173 composite dust samples. Each composite sample consists of two individual samples per indoor location, which are analyzed for Pb, As, and Cd in the field using an XRF analyzer. The composite samples are packaged and sent to an accredited laboratory for analysis of Pb, As, and Cd at a minimum. No additional indoor locations were identified where the study population spent a significant amount of time.

Dust sampling in homes and schools includes those areas where individuals spend the most time (for example. bedroom, kitchen, living room, classroom). The focus is on those individuals for whom the home survey, biological sampling, and health-outcome data will be collected.

For example, consider the four sampling scenarios in table B4.2.1. ***Important note:*** *dust sampling should occur in the same households or locations where other environmental samples are being collected and which relate to individuals providing biomonitoring and health-outcome data.*

TABLE B4.2.1 **Dust sampling scenarios**

HOUSEHOLD	INDIVIDUAL	TIME ACTIVITY	SAMPLING LOCATIONS
1	5-year-old child (female)	Bedroom, kitchen	3 wipes collected from bedroom floor and 2 wipes collected from kitchen table (1 composite)
2	6-year-old child (male)	Bedroom, kitchen, living room	3 wipes collected from the bedroom floor, 2 wipes collected from the kitchen floor, and 2 wipes collected from windowsill in living room (1 composite)
3	35-year-old mother	Bedroom, kitchen	3 wipes collected from bedroom floor and 2 wipes collected from windowsill in kitchen (1 composite)
4	10-year-old child (male)	School (classroom and lunchroom)	2 wipes collected from classroom and 2 wipes collected from lunchroom (1 composite)

Source: World Bank compilation.

different indoor areas where the population of interest spends the most time and over which activities occur (for example, bedroom, kitchen, living room). Different surfaces can be sampled for any given room (for example, floor, table, windowsill).

- Record all sampling locations on the in-field data sheets.
- The area to be sampled (that is, the area to be wiped) must be a rectangle or square (preferred) with measurable dimensions so the total surface area can be easily calculated, and either marked off with tape or using a cardboard template. It is recommended that the wipe area be at least 900 cm² (approximately 1 square foot) to obtain enough dust for analysis of Pb.
- Follow specific guidelines regarding how much pressure to apply on the wipe, how to properly fold the wipe, and what type of wipe to use. The goal is to pick up all dust from the sample area, including any debris (for example, paint chips, chunks of dust or dirt). Disposable, moistened towelettes or baby wipes (for example, GhostWipe™) are generally recommended. The wipe material should meet appropriate performance criteria.
- Use an XRF analyzer in the field to measure the dust Pb, As, and Cd concentration for each of the individual dust samples. Note that the XRF can be simultaneously calibrated for additional metals, and it may be possible to use the same instrument for both the soil and dust samples, but this will depend on manufacturer specifications.
- Combine the individual dust samples into a single composite dust sample and package and send this composite sample to an accredited laboratory for analysis.
- Follow the directions and use the sampling equipment provided or recommended by the in-field research team and analytical laboratory with respect to sample collection, preparation, and shipping, including use of such personal protective equipment as gloves.

WATER SAMPLING

Exposure pathways and routes

ULAB-recycling sites have the potential to affect local water supplies due to leaching or runoff of contaminated soil to surface water or groundwater, leaching of waste products from lagoons or pits to surface water or groundwater, or migration of contaminated surface water from wastewater discharges to other surface water sources or groundwater. Various types of surface-water sources at ULAB-recycling sites (for example, lakes, rivers, streams) and groundwater sources of various depths may therefore contain Pb, As, and Cd. Dermal contact and ingestion of contaminated water are the primary exposure routes and pathways at ULAB-recycling sites. Dermal exposures can occur when adults or children bathe, wash clothes or dishes, swim, or wade in surface-water sources or if groundwater is used for bathing or washing. Direct ingestion can occur when individuals drink water obtained from surface or groundwater sources. This latter exposure pathway is likely to be the most relevant for contributing to population exposures. Note that either surface water or groundwater (or both) can be used as sources for drinking water at ULAB-recycling sites.

Sampling protocol and analysis

Water samples should be collected at each ULAB-recycling site and reference site for each household where soil and dust samples were collected as well as other targeted locations (for example, schools) where soil or dust samples were collected, if applicable. Specifically, water samples should be collected at residences, schools, or daycare facilities where study participants spend significant amounts of time and where water is used for drinking, bathing, washing, or recreational purposes. It is important to recognize that the source of drinking water may vary for individuals within a site as well as across ULAB-recycling sites, and the collection of drinking-water samples will therefore depend on the water source and population-activity patterns. Typical sources include tap water from a municipal source (groundwater or surface water); an individual or shared household well; a communal surface-water source (for example, a lake, river, or stream); or a communal groundwater well. In some cases, multiple sources will need to be considered. Determining where to collect these samples should be informed by the refined CSM and household survey (chapters 2 and 3).

When collecting water samples, the following general guidelines should be followed (see box 4.3):

- If possible, all water samples should be collected at the individual household or targeted location (for example, school) where the water is available for consumption or use. If the source is tap water, water samples should be collected at the point of release (that is, the tap). If there is a communal water source (for example, a community well) applicable to multiple participating households, samples should be collected from the water source. Samples can also be collected directly from an off-site surface-water body if it is commonly used for recreational or other purposes (or if the in-field research team would like additional data on potential site contamination).
- Water samples should reflect the actual water being used for drinking or other purposes; therefore, if the water has undergone any type of treatment (for example, chlorination), then the treated water should be sampled.

BOX 4.3

Water sampling at a hypothetical ULAB-recycling site

Water samples are collected at those households and targeted locations (for example, schools) with independent sources of water used for drinking water, bathing, or washing or surface-water sources used for swimming, wading, or other recreational purposes. In this example, approximately half (50 percent) of households obtain water from a private well for drinking water and other activities, whereas the other half (50 percent) obtain their water directly from a central surface-water body. The targeted schools have private wells used for drinking water only. Therefore, of the 170 households that are sampled for soil and dust, a duplicate water sample is collected from 85 residences (170 ÷ 2) that have a private well. For the remaining households, a duplicate water sample is collected from the central local surface-water source. A duplicate water sample is also collected from each of the three targeted schools. ***Important note:*** *water sampling should occur in the same households or locations where other environmental samples are being collected and which relate to individuals providing biomonitoring and health-outcome data.*

- For each water sample, duplicate samples of approximately 1 liter each should be taken. The exact sample quantity should be determined with the laboratory conducting the analyses.
- Follow the directions and use the sampling equipment provided or recommended by the in-field research team and analytical laboratory with respect to sample collection, preparation, and shipping (including use of personal protective equipment, such as gloves).

AGRICULTURAL PRODUCT SAMPLING

Exposure pathways and routes

Because ULAB-recycling sites have the potential to affect local soil and water supplies, as discussed above, activities at ULAB-recycling sites may also affect locally produced agricultural products that come into contact with contaminated soil or water. In particular, contaminated irrigation water from affected surface water or groundwater sources may be used to irrigate crops. Crops may also be grown in contaminated soil or subject to aerial deposition, with resulting uptake in root systems or deposition on foliage. Additionally, animals may be grazed on contaminated soil or given contaminated water to drink. Various types of agricultural products at ULAB-recycling sites may therefore contain Pb, As, and Cd. Examples of locally produced agricultural products include fruits, vegetables, and grains; animals consumed for meat (for example, chickens, cattle); and various animal products (for example, milk, cheese, eggs). These products may be produced at multiple scales, ranging from small family gardens at the household level to large commercial operations that sell products at local or off-site markets. Direct ingestion of contaminated foodstuffs may represent an important exposure route and pathway at ULAB-recycling sites.

The data on contaminant concentrations in agricultural products (which can include fruits, vegetables, grains, dairy, meat, and eggs) are combined with information on food consumption collected as part of the household survey (chapter 3). Statistical models predicting intake or exploring correlations are used to inform how exposure factors combine with environmental concentrations and how those relate to body burdens from the biomonitoring data. Another approach for this is to analyze food consumption based on a composite sample using a duplicate diet approach. Participants consume food as they normally would over some time period—for example, 24 or 48 hours—making sure to both record what and how much of each food item they are consuming as well as putting aside a small amount of food from each snack and meal. These individual samples are combined into a composite sample and analyzed for the CoCs. This method provides detailed information on intake, and when combined with biomonitoring data, can be used to parameterize models that predict CoC concentrations in humans (for example, intake or physiologically based pharmacokinetic [PBPK] models).

Duplicate diet studies are not recommended here since the focus is on exposures occurring over longer time periods. In addition, data on CoC concentrations in agricultural products can be used to estimate population intake rates, given assumptions on consumption frequencies, and therefore represent more useful data.

Sampling protocol and analysis

Selected agricultural samples should be collected at each ULAB-recycling site and reference site for each household where soil, dust, and water samples have been collected and perhaps other targeted locations. Specifically, the only agricultural products that should be sampled are ones that are locally grown (either at the household or community level), are frequently consumed by the population of interest, and have the potential for contamination. Determining which specific agricultural products to sample at each site will require further refinement of the CSM, information obtained from the household survey, and a detailed understanding by the in-field research team of the ways in which the ULAB facility might affect local resources.

Examples of different types of foodstuffs that might be sampled at individual ULAB-recycling sites include the following:

- Rice grown in surface water affected by wastewater from ULAB activities
- Chickens foraging directly at ULAB sites (focus on sampling what is most commonly consumed—for example, chicken liver, eggs)

BOX 4.4

Agricultural sampling at a hypothetical ULAB-recycling site

Agricultural sampling should reflect products frequently consumed by individuals in the study that are affected by ULAB activities (for example, via the use of contaminated irrigation water). In this example, about half (50 percent) of the households have their own gardens, while those households located closest to the facility purchase products from a local market that are grown near the ULAB-recycling source area. Thus, agricultural samples are collected from 85 households that have home gardens, whereas additional targeted samples (2 samples each) are taken from the local market and agricultural field closest to the ULAB-recycling facility. See the sampling scenarios in table B4.4.1. ***Important note:*** *agricultural sampling should occur from the same*

households or locations where other environmental samples are being collected and which relate directly to individuals providing biomonitoring and health-outcome data. In the context of linking environmental exposures to health outcomes in an exposed population, there is limited utility to sampling products that are (a) not being consumed by individuals providing biomonitoring and health-outcome data, and (b) not affected by ULAB activities (for example, beyond the zone of influence of ULAB-waste releases and discharges). Other studies with additional objectives—for example, broader site characterization or evaluating the possibility of contaminated products being sold or used outside the study area—may benefit from broadening the scope of sampling.

TABLE B4.4.1 Agricultural product sampling scenarios

HOUSEHOLD OR SAMPLING LOCATION	INDIVIDUAL	PRODUCT SAMPLES
1	5-year-old child (female)	Local chicken liver from the refrigerator
2	6-year-old child (male)	Leafy greens from the home garden
3	35-year-old mother	Composite sample of leafy greens from the garden where soil samples were obtained
Market	Multiple households	1 leafy-green composite, 40 gr chicken liver
Agricultural field	Multiple households	1 leafy-green composite, 1 cassava composite

Source: World Bank compilation.

- Root vegetables grown in soils from backyard gardens irrigated with surface water affected by wastewater from ULAB activities
- Leafy greens grown downwind within a depositional area of ULAB activities
- Beans or other legumes grown in soils irrigated with contaminated surface water and within the depositional area of the ULAB facility.

When collecting agricultural samples, the following general guidelines should be followed (see box 4.4):

- If possible, all agricultural samples should be collected at the individual household where the foodstuff is ready or available for consumption (for example, kitchen), or taken directly from the garden for fruits and vegetables. Samples may be collected from the original source (for example, community field crop) or marketplace for commonly consumed foodstuffs that are not available at the household level (or if the in-field research team requires additional data on potential site contamination). An emphasis should be placed on samples that may be applicable to the largest number of participating households (for example, foods obtained from a market or similar source).
- For samples taken from household gardens, collect multiple samples of the same item if possible and combine as a composite sample (for example, collect a few lettuce leaves from several different heads of lettuce).
- Agricultural samples should reflect only the edible portion of foodstuffs and target those portions of the food of greatest concern (for example, green leaves, chicken liver).
- Sufficient amounts need to be collected per food sample; recommended levels typically range from 40 to 100 grams for fruits, vegetables, and meat products. The exact amount will depend on the specific laboratory requirements.
- Follow the directions and use the sampling equipment provided or recommended by the in-field research team and analytical laboratory with respect to sample collection, preparation, and shipping (including use of personal protective equipment, such as gloves).

BOX 4.5

Total environmental samples

MEDIUM	HOUSEHOLDS	OTHER LOCATIONS
Soil	170 composites (4 individual XRF) analyzed for all metals; 85 (subset of 170) analyzed for Pb and As bioavailability	3 composite samples per school (4 individual XRF) analyzed for all metals and Pb and As bioavailability
Dust	170 composites (4 individual XRF) analyzed for all metals	3 composite samples per school (4 individual XRF)
Water	85 from individual homes	3 from schools; 1 from the central shared well
Agricultural products	85 from home gardens / individual homes	4 samples from market, agricultural field
Total	510 samples	17 samples

Fish

In general, Pb, As, and Cd do not bioaccumulate in fish tissue. Therefore, sampling for these CoCs in fish tissue at ULAB sites is not recommended.

RESOURCES

See appendix C for a listing of country-specific guidelines and guidance for sampling and laboratory methods, including URLs.

REFERENCE

US EPA (US Environmental Protection Agency). N.d. *EPA Method 1340 SW-846 Test Method 1340: In Vitro Bioaccessibility Assay for Lead in Soil.* Washington, DC: US EPA. https://www .epa.gov/hw-sw846/sw-846-test-method-1340-vitro-bioaccessibility-assay-lead-soil.

5 General Guidelines for Biological Sampling

This chapter provides an overview of biological sampling conducted for each participating individual in order to provide data on both internal exposure concentrations (for example, biomonitoring) and potential health outcomes associated with exposures to the contaminants of concern (CoCs). These data are linked to household- and participant-specific environmental samples collected per the recommendations in chapter 4 and clinical health-outcome data from chapter 6.

INTRODUCTION

Biological samples provide the best evidence of combined exposure to CoCs from all sources and exposure pathways or routes at each used lead-acid battery (ULAB) site. The biological sampling data will also be used to confirm or validate estimates of CoC exposure based on the exposure-factor data (chapter 3) and environmental-sampling data (chapter 4) collected at each site. That is, the goal is to avoid collecting biological samples at future sites if less intrusive exposure-factor data and environmental data can be collected that are sufficiently predictive of total exposures. Additionally, as discussed in chapter 6, biological samples will be analyzed for possible indicators of health outcomes or nutritional and health status. This chapter provides general guidelines for what types of biological samples should be collected for each contaminant and recommended approaches for sample collection. Important factors that will need to be considered on a site-by-site basis are also noted. Detailed protocols and procedures for collecting a biological sample, handling and preparing biological samples, and laboratory analysis of biological samples are not addressed here and will be the final responsibility of the in-field research team and associated trained professionals (although some useful resources are presented in appendix D). It is essential that the biological sampling be conducted for the same individuals for whom the household survey (chapter 3), environmental (chapter 4), and health-outcome (chapter 6) data are collected. The same type of biological samples should also be collected from both the identified ULAB sites and matched reference sites. Note that any necessary ethical clearances will need to be obtained prior to sample collection by the in-field research team.

The key factors to consider when evaluating potential biomarkers include (a) how well the biomarker correlates with the dose (or external exposure) to appropriate forms of the contaminant, for example, arsenic (As) versus organic As); (b) how well the biomarker correlates with the contaminant concentration in tissue relative to the health outcome; (c) how well the biomarker measurement correlates with changes in the effective dose at the target tissue over time; (d) an understanding of the cultural characteristics of the population; (e) technology availability; and (f) invasiveness of the sample collection.

Because the goal of the biological sampling design is to both (a) quantify the magnitude of exposure among individual population members to each CoC at ULAB sites, and (b) to identify potential subclinical evidence of disease that could be associated with exposures to these contaminants, the biological sampling should attempt to provide the most accurate and relevant data on biomarkers of exposure or biomarkers of effect for each CoC (and also provide standard information on nutritional and health status). Biological sampling matrices can include urine, blood, toenails, and hair. Breast milk and cord blood are additional matrices but are not recommended in this study due to the limited utility in relating exposure to health outcomes for an infant population. Each of these matrices offers advantages and limitations depending on the contaminant, health outcome or intermediate health outcome, and biomarker to be measured. An emphasis is placed on point-of-care methods (for example, comparable to in-field for environmental sampling) that provide rapid immunoassay-based results.

BIOLOGICAL SAMPLING MATRICES

Biomarkers of exposure are measurements in biological matrices that reflect the total absorbed or internal dose of a contaminant from all sources and exposure routes and pathways. In some cases, metabolites as opposed to parent compounds may provide the most reliable measures of exposure. Biological sampling matrices can include urine, blood, toenails, and hair. Breast milk and cord blood are additional matrices but are not recommended here due to the invasiveness of data collection and limited utility in relating exposure to health outcomes for an infant population. Each of these matrices offers advantages and limitations depending on the contaminant and biomarker to be measured.

The following sections summarize potential biomarkers of exposure specific to each CoC. Because several biological media are possible for each CoC, each of which has advantages and limitations, a hierarchy of preferred options is presented in color-coded tables, as defined in table 5.1.

Lead

Lead (Pb) is the primary CoC at ULAB sites. Whole blood (not serum blood) is the most reliable biological matrix for evaluating Pb exposures. Venous blood samples collected by a trained medical professional and submitted to an accredited laboratory are considered the gold standard for Pb analysis. Somewhat less reliable, but also less invasive, is a dried blood spot collected as a capillary blood sample in-field and sent to a laboratory. Finally, an in-field testing instrument (that is,

TABLE 5.1 **Hierarchy of preferred biomarkers of exposure**

Gold standard. This biomarker has been well vetted in the literature with one or more validated, cost-effective laboratory methods with high levels of precision. This is the preferred biomarker given the primary research objectives in this document.
Screening level. This biomarker is an appropriate default for low-resource applications. It is the least invasive, lowest cost, typically with in-field analysis. However, only the total metal can be measured and will have high detection levels and may not have the precision to evaluate statistical associations with outcomes.
Low preference. This biomarker (white color) can be used as a last resort but is generally not preferred due to limitations with respect to associations (that is, they are not the best measure of exposure or predictive of outcomes based on literature studies).
To be avoided. This biomarker is not appropriate since it does not measure the exposure of interest, is expensive, or does not have a validated method.

Source: World Bank compilation.

TABLE 5.2 **Overview of biomarkers of exposure for Pb**

BIOLOGICAL MATRIX AND CONTAMINANT	ADVANTAGES	LIMITATIONS	CAN MATRIX BE USED TO EVALUATE HEALTH OUTCOME?
Lead			
Venous blood	Well-vetted, standardized routine analysis with highest precision and reliability	Requires medical professional; requirements for processing, storage, handling	Can do complete blood count and metabolic panel; additional markers related to anemia
Capillary blood (including dried blood spot)	LeadCare in-field analyzer; immediate results. Alternatively, can use dried blood spot and send to laboratory. Dried blood spot shows high variability compared to venous blood	Pb only; shows higher variability compared to venous blood sample sent to laboratory. Field conditions may compromise ability to measure accurately	HemoCue in-field for hemoglobin (anemia) as marker of potential intermediate effect. Can measure calcium
Urine	No advantages other than being less invasive	Can be used but not preferred	Standard renal panel (for example, albumin, proteinuria) as marker for renal damage—can use spot sample
Hair	No advantages other than being less invasive	Can be used but not preferred; reflects direct contact of hair with dust rather than absorbed exposure	No relevant outcome measurement
Toenail/ fingernail	Least invasive; lowest cost and immediate results in-field using XRF. No specific storage or transport requirements. Provides information on short-term and long-term exposures	High detection levels. Needs to be correlated with blood levels. LeadCare in-field always preferred	No relevant outcome measurement

Source: World Bank compilation.

LeadCare analyzer) calibrated for Pb can be used to collect a capillary blood sample, with immediate documentation of the results in a computer or on field-data sheets. The least-cost and lowest-resource-intensive choice is an in-field XRF analyzer to analyze toenail samples, but detection levels will be higher, with greater variability in results. Urine and hair samples are the least reliable biological matrices for evaluating Pb exposures and should generally be avoided for this purpose. A test for chronic Pb exposures in adults is the zinc protoporphyrin (ZPP) blood test, which is recommended by both the Secretariat of the Basel Convention (2003) and the Occupational Health and Safety Administration (OSHA) in the United States to evaluate long-term Pb exposures in adults. It is not typically suitable for children, however, since it reflects exposures over longer time periods. Table 5.2 provides an overview of the advantages and limitations of different biological matrices for sampling Pb. The final column is used to identify whether the matrix is useful for additionally capturing a biomarker of effect (for example, obviating the need for additional sample collection).

Arsenic

The best measure of arsenic (As) exposure is the metabolite monomethylarsonic acid (%MMA) obtained from a speciated creatinine-adjusted urine sample. Although this method requires a separate laboratory analysis (for example, high-performance liquid chromatography [HPLC] with hydride atomic absorption spectrometry [HG-AAS] or inductively coupled plasma mass spectrometry [ICP-MS] or similar), it is a widely used measure of exposure in epidemiological studies. It is also more often associated with health outcomes than measures of total As. An in-field XRF analyzer can be used to analyze toenail samples for As, although this is a much less robust approach. Blood and hair samples are the least reliable biological matrices for evaluating As exposures and should generally be avoided for this purpose. Table 5.3 provides an overview of the advantages and limitations of different biological matrices for sampling As.

TABLE 5.3 **Overview of biomarkers of exposure for As**

BIOLOGICAL MATRIX AND CONTAMINANT	ADVANTAGES	LIMITATIONS	CAN MATRIX BE USED TO EVALUATE HEALTH OUTCOME?
Arsenic			
Venous blood	Can use the same sample to evaluate intermediate outcomes	Not considered reliable; clearance of As is rapid. Time between exposure and sampling critical. Seafood sources greatly influence blood levels	Can do complete blood count, assays for pre-cancerous marker (for example, DNA adduct formation, micronucleus formation)
Capillary blood (for example, dried blood spot)	Not as invasive as venous blood; samples can be collected by nonmedical personnel. Storage and transport significantly simplified	Still has to be sent to a laboratory; sample volume can be an issue. Not considered reliable for As given rapid clearance. Time between exposure and sampling critical. Seafood sources greatly influence levels. Does not show good correlation with split-sample venous blood	Can measure hemoglobin, calcium in-field but these have not been associated with As effects
Urine	Less expensive to measure total As. Can measure multiple metals using the same method	Total As does not always predict outcomes; associations not statistically significant. May do better collecting toenail	Standard renal panel (for example, albumin, proteinuria) as marker for renal damage. If collecting for speciated As, then only requires small additional volume. Can also use spot sample or dipstick
Speciated urine	%MMA shows consistent relationship with lung, skin, bladder cancer from oral exposures. Can use same sample for standard renal panel; creatinine	More expensive than total As; analysis is unique to As	Standard renal panel
Hair	No advantages other than less invasive	Does not reflect internal / absorbed dose; reflects external exposures	No relevant outcome measurement
Toenail/ fingernail	Least invasive, lowest cost and immediate results in-field if using XRF. No specific storage or transport requirements. Provides information on short- and long-term exposures	High detection levels. Measures total As. Random within-person exposure variability leads to attenuation of measures of association between exposure and outcome	No relevant outcome measurement

Source: World Bank compilation.

TABLE 5.4 **Overview of biomarkers of exposure for Cd**

BIOLOGICAL MATRIX AND CONTAMINANT	ADVANTAGES	LIMITATIONS	CAN MATRIX BE USED TO EVALUATE HEALTH OUTCOME?
Cadmium			
Venous blood	No advantages	Reflects only recent exposures. Meta-analyses show no association with outcomes. Invasive sample	Focus is on renal effects; urine more useful
Capillary blood (for example, dried blood spot)	No advantages other than somewhat less invasive than a venous sample	Reflects only recent exposures. Meta-analyses show no association with outcomes	Focus is on renal effects; urine more useful
Urine	Most widely used and well-vetted. Recommended by WHO, US EPA. Not invasive. Measures long-term low-level exposure. Can use spot sample	Moderately invasive; requires urine sample	Standard renal panel (for example, albumin, proteinuria) as marker for renal damage; can use spot sample for albumin alone
Hair	No advantages other than less invasive	Not recommended	No relevant outcome measurement
Toenail/fingernail	Least invasive, lowest cost; can use XRF in-field. No specific storage or transport requirements. Provides information on short-term and long-term exposures	High detection levels for XRF. Does not correlate well with urine levels. Not associated with renal outcomes. Can be difficult to obtain required sample mass	No relevant outcome measurement

Source: World Bank compilation.

Cadmium

Given that cadmium (Cd) affects the renal system, the best exposure metric is creatine-adjusted urine, which provides the most appropriate measure of Cd exposures and has been widely used in many epidemiological studies. Table 5.4 provides an overview of the advantages and limitations of different biological matrices for sampling Cd.

BIOLOGICAL SAMPLING PROTOCOL

The collection of biological samples should be done in conjunction with the household survey (chapter 3) and evaluation of health outcomes (chapter 6). As noted earlier, the selection of biological-sampling methods emphasizes rapid, less invasive, in-field approaches where possible, recognizing that samples sent to a laboratory represent the "gold standard." Standardized guidelines exist for collecting biological samples (see appendix D for examples of specific guidelines from the United States Centers for Disease Control, World Health Organization, and others) and the in-field team should be trained in those or rely on local medical professionals.

When collecting and analyzing biological samples, the following general guidelines should be followed:

• When collecting blood samples, particularly capillary blood samples, the skin must first be thoroughly washed and dried to avoid contamination. This is a common problem encountered during field studies of this kind.

• If collecting a dried blood spot, discard the first drop. Contamination is very likely when collecting these samples. Follow all laboratory guidelines and protocols.

- When collecting toenail samples, it may be possible to use the same XRF analyzer as is used for the soil and dust sampling, but this instrument will require a separate calibration and samples cannot be collected simultaneously. Thus, it may be more appropriate to have multiple XRF devices to address multiple purposes.
- When collecting urine samples, the first morning void is preferred because it is generally more concentrated. This will require some planning to obtain a sample during this time period. Note that 24-hour urine samples may be too cumbersome to collect and spot urine samples may be less robust.
- If the same venous blood or urine samples will be used to assess indicators of nutrient status or health outcomes, greater sample volumes of whole blood or urine may be needed.
- For both blood and urine samples, stringent guidelines related to the preservation and transportation of biological samples must be followed.
- Urine samples should be adjusted for creatinine levels to account for dilution-dependent sample variation in urine concentrations (that is, individuals who are well hydrated will have more diluted urinary concentrations of environmental contaminants).

RESOURCES

See appendix D for a listing of relevant resources related to biomonitoring, including recommended methods and guidance from health agencies, and specific testing protocols.

6 General Guidelines for Assessing Health Outcomes

This chapter provides general guidelines for collecting health-outcome data based on a combination of possible approaches, including self-reported health status and medical histories that can be administered by nonmedical personnel, medical examinations and biological sampling conducted by health professionals, and diagnostic screening tools related to specific health outcomes that might be administered by a physician or psychologist. The exact approach to be followed at each site will depend on participant access to health care facilities (where examinations and screenings are likely to occur); availability of in-field methods (for surveys, exams, sample collection, or other tools that can be implemented onsite); and researcher access to validated, culturally sensitive diagnostic tools. Health-outcome data will be collected from individuals within the households identified for sampling in chapter 3. The same health-outcome data should be collected from individuals at both the identified used lead-acid battery (ULAB) sites and matched reference sites to evaluate differences that may be attributable to differences in contaminant of concern (CoC) exposures. Note that any necessary ethical and institutional review board (IRB) clearances will need to be obtained prior to data collection.

INTRODUCTION

There are three categories of possible health outcomes that can be measured. The first is a medical diagnosis related to direct or measurable clinical outcomes known to be associated with exposure to the CoC of interest—for example, bladder cancer or hyperkeratosis associated with arsenic (As) exposures, and cognitive deficits as measured by age-specific standardized testing instruments associated with exposures to lead (Pb) and As. The second is an intermediate, nonspecific observation or measurement associated with the health outcome of interest—for example, increased blood pressure associated with cardiovascular outcomes that may be related to exposure to Pb and cadmium (Cd). The third is an intermediate biochemical measurement (that is, biomarker of effect) that requires laboratory or in-field analysis of a biological matrix—for example, diagnosis of anemia based on hematocrit level in blood that may be related to Pb exposures, and micronucleus formation in blood that may be associated with genotoxic effects of As.

It should be noted that biomonitoring is a rapidly expanding field with improvements in molecular techniques leading to the identification of novel biomarkers, including oncogenes, tumor-suppressor genes, microRNAs and long non-coding RNAs, DNA methylation, and others. The evolving discipline of "omics," including proteomics and genomics, has led to the identification of genetic and epigenetic alterations, typically based on blood samples and utilizing various laboratory-based assays. These methods are not yet mature enough to be recommended for routine use in low- and middle-income countries (LMICs) but could be considered in the future. A key drawback at the current time is the requirement for specialized laboratory equipment, invasiveness of biological sampling (typically a venous blood sample is required), and the increased expense of such analyses.

Although it would be desirable to measure unique health outcomes associated with exposures to each CoC from one or more of these categories, a key challenge of this type of investigation is that the primary CoCs from ULAB sites (for example, Pb, As, and Cd) as well as other factors share common biological targets, so it is difficult to discern the relative contribution, if any, of each CoC exposure to the identified health outcome. For example, exposure to multiple CoCs has been associated with cognitive and neurodevelopmental outcomes in children using age-specific standardized instruments (for example, Bayley Scale of Infant Development or IQ tests). Additionally, intermediate measures of health outcomes in the absence of overt toxicity (biomarkers of effect) may show associations with exposure concentrations as measured through biomonitoring (chapter 5) or environmental concentrations of CoCs (chapter 4). Therefore, it is important to note that while biomarkers of exposure are CoC-specific, biomarkers of effect may not be CoC-specific. Moreover, there are many other factors that could influence the same health outcomes associated with these CoCs, ranging from such lifestyle factors as diet, exercise, and smoking status to such common environmental exposures as air pollution. It is anticipated that these latter factors will be captured during the household survey and subsequently controlled for through statistical analyses of the data.

Given these constraints, the primary goal of these guidelines is to try to collect enough information about direct and indirect health outcomes from each participant to evaluate (a) differences in these outcomes between the ULAB-exposed population and a nonexposed reference population; and (b) possible relationships between measured environmental concentrations (chapter 4), biomarkers of exposure (chapter 5), and health outcomes at the individual level.

SELF-REPORTED HEALTH STATUS AND MEDICAL HISTORY

Each participant should provide basic health-related information, including the following:

- Age, weight, and body mass index
- Smoking status
- Alcohol consumption

- Physical activity
- Medication use (for example, antihypertensive)
- Medical diagnoses and dates of diagnosis, including high blood pressure, chronic illnesses such as cancer or kidney disease, or any other medical or mental health conditions. If the medical history is for a child under the age of 18, a parent or caregiver will likely need to provide this information
- Health status relative to any known deficiencies (for example, rickets, pyorrhea), particularly in children, including symptoms such as bleeding gums
- Past and present illnesses, whether formally diagnosed or not, and dates: information on any serious or chronic illnesses the person has experienced—for instance, if the individual has ever had tuberculosis or if the individual has asthma or diabetes
- Family medical history: information on any diagnosed health conditions of immediate family members (for example, parents, siblings), including conditions such as cancer, heart disease, and mental illnesses.

This information can be obtained in-field as part of the household survey (see appendix B and the questions starting with number 4 in the Example of a Household Questionnaire). Alternatively, if a medical examination will be conducted, a more complete medical history (for example, see Bickley 2012) can be obtained under the supervision of a medical professional, which is likely to provide more detailed and refined data based on clinical observations.

MEDICAL EXAMS AND BIOLOGICAL TESTING

Selected health outcomes can be measured using direct observation or testing, some of which (for example, blood pressure) may be accomplished by nonmedical personnel in the field, while others may require specific training for nonmedical professionals (for example, arsenicosis versus a generalized skin rash) or even a more formal medical diagnosis.

Biological sampling may also provide useful information about potential health impacts or precursor effects. *Biomarkers of effect* are measurements in biological matrices that serve as an indicator of a specific health outcome or preclinical (upstream) change or effect at the molecular or cellular level or have been shown to reliably predict health outcomes. These measurements are typically obtained from standard blood or urine tests, such as complete blood count (CBC), or standard renal panel. Although most biomarkers of effect are nonspecific with respect to exposure (that is, it is not possible to discern the source of the observed biomarker or whether it is attributed to the contaminants of interest), they can serve as potential indicators for the health outcome of interest. However, it is important to recognize that upstream or precursor effects may not lead to downstream outcomes or permanent effects. Biomarkers of effect can therefore provide useful (although not definitive) information and indicators on the continuum from exposure to overt health outcome. Table 6.1 provides an overview of the recommended biomarkers of effect (including nutritional and health status), with an emphasis on lower-cost, point-of-care, and in-field approaches, followed by a discussion of each proposed biomarker by category of health outcome.

TABLE 6.1 **Overview of recommended biomarkers of effect**

BIOMARKER	SAMPLING APPROACH	PURPOSE	NOTES
ALA (aminolevulinic acid)	24-hour urine	Impacts associated with acute Pb poisoning	Not as useful for chronic Pb exposures
Proteinuria	Reagent strip point-of-care testing device; dipstick	Renal effects (Cd, Pb)	Total protein in urine
Albumin	Reagent strip point-of-care testing device; dipstick	Renal effects; microalbuminuria noted as sensitive biomarker with respect to renal outcomes (Cd, Pb)	Predominant protein found in urine
β2-m (urinary β2-micro-globulin)	Used with serum creatinine to evaluate glomerular filtration rate (GFR)	Nonspecific urinary biomarker of early proximal tubule effects (Cd)	Selected by European Food Safety Authority (EFSA) as preferred biomarker of effect for Cd
Glomerular filtration rate (GFR)	Urine; can be calculated by laboratory or from albumin, creatinine, height, weight	Predictive measure of progressive renal dysfunction. (Cd, Pb)	Standard equations not appropriate for children; see text. Use Gao et al. 2013.
Creatinine	Serum; can use dried blood spot	Necessary for GFR estimating equations (Cd, Pb)	
Creatinine	Requires urine sample (no dipstick)	Necessary to adjust for urine volume	Needed for biomarkers of exposure in urine
25hydroxyvitamin D$_3$ (25(OH)D$_3$)	May be possible infield	Vitamin D deficiency, micronutrient status	Vemulapati et al. 2017.
Calcium	Standard renal panel; may be in-field method	Health status, micronutrient status	
Hemoglobin	Complete blood count in laboratory; in-field HemoCue	Measures anemic status (Pb), also affects absorption of metals generally	Complete blood count from a venous sample provides additional markers such as hematocrit, platelet count, corpuscular volume, and so forth
C-reactive protein	Dried blood spot; may be a rapid point-of-care method	Inflammatory biomarker; associated with lung health (As) and cardiovascular outcomes (Pb)	See appendix D for references and links to point-of-care C-reactive protein (CRP) methods
DNA adduct formation	Should be possible to use dried blood spot sent to lab	Associated with carcinogenic outcomes (As, Cd)	Recommended by the IPCS
Micronucleus formation	Should be possible to use dried blood spot sent to lab	Associated with carcinogenic outcomes (As, Cd)	Recommended by the IPCS

Source: World Bank compilation.

Renal effects

Urinary and serum enzymes and low molecular weight (LMW) proteins have been used as early markers of kidney dysfunction and are useful for the detection of small changes in the function of tubular epithelial cells predictive of many pathological conditions. Enzyme and protein excretion increases before elevation of other markers of renal function, such as creatinine, and well before overt disease. Enzyme excretion rates in urine or blood are elevated following release from cells damaged by exposure to exogenous substances such as CoCs, or from regenerating cells that lead to increased enzyme induction. LMW proteins are freely filtered across the glomerular capillary wall and almost completely reabsorbed by the proximal tubular cells. Functional or structural damage from exposure to CoCs can lead to reduced reabsorption in the proximal tubule, leading to increases in proteins in both blood and urine. These biomarkers are associated with exposures to Cd and Pb.

Proteinuria

Proteinuria is a classic early sign of kidney dysfunction and, although reversible, its presence carries important prognostic information. Proteinuria is typically measured as total protein and can be evaluated rapidly in-field using a reagent strip in a spot urine sample. Early morning void is preferred, and urinary creatinine should be measured concurrently. Validated in-field or point-of-care assays exist, but sending urine samples to a laboratory for a standard renal panel will always yield more information—for example, albumin, BUN (blood urea nitrogen) /creatinine ratio (calculated), calcium, carbon dioxide, chloride, creatinine, estimated glomerular filtration rate (calculated), glucose, phosphate, potassium, sodium, and BUN. Proteinuria can be measured as total protein or albumin (microalbuminuria), which has been an excellent predictor of kidney function and is the preferred biomarker.

β2-m (urinary β2-microglobulin) is a urinary biomarker recommended by the European Food Safety Authority (EFSA) biomonitoring program for evaluating intermediate effects associated with Cd exposures, but may also reflect effects from renal-acting agents other than the CoCs of interest at ULAB sites.

Glomerular filtration rate (GFR)

The best measure of kidney function is the glomerular filtration rate (GFR), which reflects potential dysfunction and exposures in different areas of the kidney as compared to proteinuria. However, measuring GFR can be challenging and is therefore typically estimated from a blood sample by using equations (eGFR) based on the plasma concentration of creatinine or cystatin C, another common protein. Well-vetted standardized equations exist for adults based on height, weight, and serum creatinine, but these are not appropriate for use in children. To estimate GFR in children, the recommendation is to use a set of equations, as developed by Gao et al. (2013) and available as a stand-alone online calculator as endorsed by the International Society of Nephrology.

Cardiovascular effects

Potential cardiovascular effects associated with exposure to CoCs found at ULAB sites can vary from atherosclerosis to myocardial infarction to ischemic events broadly referred to as cardiovascular disease (CVD). C-reactive protein (CRP) is a blood biomarker of inflammation shown to be predictive of a range of cardiovascular outcomes. While not as sensitive or as specific as homocysteine, CRP can be measured using in-field assays, and has also been shown to be predictive of chronic kidney disease and chronic obstructive pulmonary disease (COPD). Individuals with COPD face a two to five times greater risk of developing lung cancer, a key outcome associated with As exposures. Thus, CRP, while nonspecific, may be indicative of intermediate health outcomes associated with exposure to CoCs at ULAB sites.

Recently, bioactive molecules such as asymmetric dimethylarginine (ADMA) and adipocyte fatty acid-binding protein (FABP4, also known as aP2 and AFABP) have emerged as new predictive biomarkers of CVD and have also been associated with blood Pb levels. In the future, these may be considered in lieu of CRP.

Carcinogenic effects

Exposures to As and Cd are associated with carcinogenic outcomes, including lung, skin, and kidney cancers. Although the household survey (chapter 3) includes a set of questions on health status, it is unlikely enough cases will be observed to draw statistically meaningful conclusions, particularly given the emphasis on selecting children from each participating household. Therefore, a potential biomarker in the absence of disease may be indicative of changes at the cellular level that are predictive of carcinogenic outcomes.

The International Programme on Chemical Safety has published guidelines online to provide concise guidance on the planning, performance, and interpretation of studies to monitor groups or individuals exposed to genotoxic agents. Based on those guidelines, DNA adduct formation or micronucleus formation are two standardized assays that provide important prognostic information on exposure to potential carcinogens, including As and Cd.

CoC-specific health outcomes

The following sub sections describe the primary health outcomes associated with each CoC and recommended methods for evaluating them using medical exams and biological sampling. Appendix A provides a brief toxicity profile for each CoC, as well as links to detailed toxicological profiles developed by the US EPA, WHO, and others.

Lead

The key health outcomes associated with exposure to Pb include cognitive and neurodevelopmental effects in children, as demonstrated through performance on age-specific, culturally relevant standardized testing instruments (see the section on neurodevelopmental and cognitive testing).

A secondary, nonspecific health outcome for Pb includes effects on the renal system, which can be evaluated using nonspecific biomarkers of effect measured using in-field approaches, at a minimum, and sent to a laboratory for the most reliable, precise results. These effects on the renal system may ultimately lead to cardiovascular outcomes. A key nonspecific risk factor for cardiovascular outcomes that may also reflect increasing renal damage is blood pressure, which is easy to measure in-field or at a health care facility. In addition, there are related biomarkers that are predictive of clinical health outcomes and associated with intermediate outcomes, including C-reactive protein and protein in the urine (proteinuria; typically measured using albumin levels). Anemic status is also significant and can be measured using in-field methods such as HemoCue. Anemia may be related to health outcomes and may also influence Pb absorption.

Recommendations:

- Measure blood pressure in adults in the field or as part of a medical examination
- Measure specific biomarkers, including proteinuria (for example, albumin, ALA); anemia status (for example, hematocrit); and cardiovascular risk (for example, C-reactive protein)
- Conduct age-specific, culturally relevant cognitive testing for each child (see the sub section "Neurodevelopmental and Cognitive Testing" in this chapter).

Arsenic

Exposure to As has been associated with a number of health outcomes, including skin cancer, bladder cancer, lung cancer, neurodevelopmental health outcomes in children, and arsenicosis. Because skin is a primary target for As, hyperpigmentation and hyperkeratosis can be early symptoms of As exposures and are often first seen on the feet, hands, and palms. Figure 6.1 provides an overview of the primary dermatological signs and symptoms induced by As.

Table 6.2 provides an overview of the health outcomes that have been associated with exposure to As and recommended assessment methods.

Recommendations:

- Conduct age-specific, culturally relevant cognitive testing for each child.
- Conduct in-field screening for keratosis on the soles of the feet as part of the household survey (appendix B) or as part of a more formal medical examination.
- If keratosis is observed, consider a carcinogenic biomarker such as DNA adduct assay or micronucleus formation assay.
- Measure C-reactive protein as a nonspecific biomarker of intermediate effects on the renal and cardiovascular systems.

FIGURE 6.1

Dermatological outcomes associated with As exposures

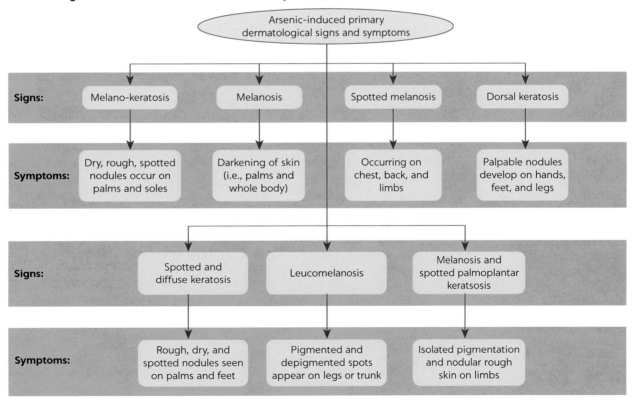

Source: Adapted from Abdul et al. 2015, figure 3.

TABLE 6.2 **Health outcomes associated with As exposures**

HEALTH OUTCOME	INTERMEDIATE HEALTH OUTCOME OR DIAGNOSTIC TEST	NONSPECIFIC BIOMARKER OF EFFECT
Arsenicosis – (may be present in children) precursor to squamous cell carcinoma in adults	Keratosis on the soles of the feet	Not applicable
Lung cancer	Lung-function tests	DNA adduct formation; micronucleus formation
Chronic pulmonary obstructive disease	Lung-function tests	C-reactive protein (CRP); predictor of forced expiratory volume
Heart disease (in adults)	Blood pressure	CRP
Cognitive and neurodevelopmental effects on children	Age-specific, culturally relevant standardized test	Not applicable

Source: World Bank compilation.

Cadmium

The most significant health outcome associated with exposures to Cd is a variety of renal effects, starting with proteinuria, leading to kidney disease, and ultimately an increased risk of kidney cancer. In the absence of outright disease or decreased kidney function, a number of well-vetted biomarkers exist for evaluating intermediate outcomes associated with Cd exposures. These include β2-m (urinary β2-microglobulin), a urinary biomarker recommended by the European Food Safety Administration, WHO, and others as the most sensitive and appropriate biomarker of Cd effects, as well as measures of kidney function, including glomerular filtration rate (GFR), which can either be measured from a standard urinary panel or calculated from protein markers measured with rapid in-field assays. In addition, there are carcinogenic biomarkers that should be considered in participants with elevated β2-m levels, including assays for DNA adduct formation and micronucleus formation.

Recommendations:

• Measure sensitive urinary biomarkers, including β2-m (urinary β2-microglobulin), and glomerular filtration rate (GFR).
• If elevated, consider measuring additional carcinogenic biomarkers, such as DNA adduct formation or micronucleus formation.

Diagnostic screening tools

As with biomarkers of effect, there are non unique intermediate health outcomes that may be both indicative of exposure to CoCs and apply to more than one CoC. For example, neurodevelopmental and cognitive outcomes in children are associated with exposures to Pb, As, and to a lesser extent Cd.

Pulmonary-function testing (PFT)

Lung cancer is a known health outcome associated with As exposures. While it may not be possible to observe cancer cases, particularly in young participants, simple lung-function tests that can be administered in-field may suggest effects on the lung that indicate increased risk of other outcomes. Decreased lung function may be an intermediate indicator of exposures to As and may provide an indication of increased risk of other adverse health outcomes. Standard lung-function tests are noninvasive tests that show how well the lungs are working. The following standardized tests measure lung volume, capacity, rates of flow, and gas exchange:

- Tidal volume (VT). This is the amount of air inhaled or exhaled during normal breathing.
- Minute volume (MV). This is the total amount of air exhaled per minute.
- Vital capacity (VC). This is the total volume of air that can be exhaled after inhaling as much as possible.
- Functional residual capacity (FRC). This is the amount of air left in the lungs after exhaling normally.
- Residual volume. This is the amount of air left in the lungs after exhaling as much as possible.
- Total lung capacity. This is the total volume of the lungs when filled with as much air as possible.
- Forced vital capacity (FVC). This is the amount of air exhaled forcefully and quickly after inhaling as much as possible.
- Forced expiratory volume (FEV). This is the amount of air expired during the first, second, and third seconds of the FVC test.
- Forced expiratory flow (FEF). This is the average rate of flow during the middle half of the FVC test.
- Peak expiratory flow rate (PEFR). This is the fastest rate at which air can be forced out of the lungs.

A variety of inexpensive peak-flow meters (one size for younger children and a larger size for older children and adults) exist to measure FEV, FVC, and FEF. Flow meters can be utilized in the field and do not require a medical professional but do require training prior to use. The following guidelines are based on best practices:

- Before each use of the meter, make sure the sliding marker or arrow is at the bottom of the numbered scale (for example, zero or the lowest number on the scale).
- Make sure the participant is standing up straight and have the participant remove gum or any food from her or his mouth. Have the participant take in as deep a breath as possible and put the peak-flow meter in the participant's mouth. Make sure her or his tongue is not on the mouthpiece. In one breath, have the participant blow out as hard and as quickly as possible. This should not be a slow exhalation but rather a fast, hard blast until nearly all of the air has been removed from the lungs.
- The force of the air exhaled from the lungs causes the marker to move along the numbered scale. Record the number.
- Repeat the entire routine three times. In general, when all three exhalations are relatively close, this is an indication that the test is being performed correctly.
- Record the highest of the three results. Do not calculate an average. It is never possible to breathe out too much when using the peak-flow meter, but it is possible to exhale too little.

Recommendations:

- Measure FEV, FVC, and FEF for each participant using a peak-flow meter. This can be done in-field.
- Measure C-reactive protein, an inflammation biomarker predictive of FEV and respiratory, cardiovascular, and renal outcomes.

Neurodevelopmental and cognitive testing

A key outcome of exposure to Pb, As, and to some extent Cd, includes neurodevelopmental and cognitive health impacts, particularly in young children. Methods to assess child development include the following:

- Direct assessment using standardized approaches by a trained medical professional in a clinical environment
- Verbal reporting or completion of a questionnaire by parents or teachers
- Unstructured observation by a trained professional in a familiar environment (for example, at home or school).

Direct assessment using standardized approaches is the preferred approach, since parental reporting may be subject to recall bias. Unstructured observation, although carried out by a professional, is difficult to reproduce, interpret, and compare to other results.

Direct assessment using standardized tests is used to evaluate a range of outcomes, including cognitive development; expressive and receptive language; fine-motor and gross-motor development; academic performance (for example, math, reading comprehension); and intelligence quotient (IQ). The specific approach chosen depends on the availability of an appropriate age-specific instrument. Results are scaled to a standardized, normative metric. Results can also be expressed as percentile ranks relative to the standardization sample. In general, normative populations for neurodevelopmental tests have been based on Western or developed countries, which is of limited utility in an LMIC context. Developmental assessments of children in LMICs face challenges due to socioeconomic, cultural, and language differences in the populations being tested. This leads to the necessity for adapting tests designed for one context and makes it difficult to compare results across countries.

The testing protocol that is selected must demonstrate internal consistency, interobserver agreement, test-retest reliability, sensitivity to maturational changes, and the ability to identify relevant outcomes. These tests must be administered by trained medical professionals (for example, child psychologists). Therefore, it is important to select a testing protocol that has been validated for the context in which it is being applied. The World Bank recently published a toolkit that provides a practical "how-to" guide for selecting and adapting of child development measurements for use in LMICs (Fernald et al. 2017). The toolkit proposes a step-by-step process to select, adapt, implement, and analyze early childhood development data. The ECD Measurement Inventory accompanies the toolkit and contains 147 measurement tools for children under 8 years. For each test, it reports the domains assessed, age range for which the tool is appropriate, method of administration, purpose of the assessment, origin and locations of use, logistics, and cost. This guide, and other, similar guides (discussed in appendix E), should be consulted (for example, http://documents.worldbank.org/curated/en/384681513101293811/pdf/WB-SIEF-ECD-MEASUREMENT-TOOLKIT.pdf) in conjunction with a trained professional on the in-field research team.

The following guidelines should be considered in selecting which testing protocol to use:

- Consultation with a medical professional with demonstrated experience in LMIC settings. It is important to include a researcher with experience in administering neurodevelopmental tests, particularly in an LMIC context. Familiarity with specific testing protocols should be emphasized.
- Time availability and conditions under which testing is to be conducted. A key consideration is how much time will be made available to administer each test. In general, a comprehensive battery of neurodevelopmental testing takes several hours and requires a clinical setting (for example, quiet, no distractions, stress-free, and so forth).
- Cultural relevance. The test must be appropriate for the cultural context and age of the child, and the test must be acceptable to the local population.
- Availability of normative data. The testing protocol should have a standardized, normative reference to evaluate the results in a consistent and comparable way.
- Consideration of comorbidities. Stress, malnutrition and nutritional status generally, low socioeconomic status, maternal education, and general household culture (for example, excessive alcohol use, smoking, drugs, and so forth) have all been associated with performance on developmental tests, and these should be noted as part of the background information on the individual being tested.

RESOURCES

Appendix E provides additional resources and weblinks for assessing health outcomes.

REFERENCES

Abdul, Khaja Shameem Mohammed, Sudheera Sammanthi Jayasinghe, Ediriweera P. S. Chandana, Channa Jayasumana, and P. Mangala C. S. De Silva. 2015. "Arsenic and Human Health Effects: A Review." *Environ. Toxicol. Pharmacol.* 40 (3): 828–46. doi:10.1016/j.etap.2015.09.016.

Bickley, L. S. 2012. *Bates' Guide to Physical Examination and History Taking*, 11th ed. Philadelphia: Lippincott Williams & Wilkins, an imprint of Wolters Kluwer.

Fernald, Lia C. H., Elizabeth Prado, Patricia Kariger, Abbie Raikes. 2017. *A Toolkit for Measuring Early Childhood Development in Low- and Middle-Income Countries*. Strategic Impact Evaluation Fund. Washington, DC: World Bank.

Gao, Anja, F. Cachat, M. Faouzi, B. J. Meyrat, E. Girardin, and Hassib Chehade. 2013. "Comparison of the Glomerular Filtration Rate in Children by the New Revised Schwartz Formula and New Generalized Formula." *Kidney International* 83 (3): 524–30.

Vemulapati, S., E. Rey, D. O'Dell, S. Mehta, and D. Erickson. 2017. "A Quantitative Point-of-Need Assay for the Assessment of Vitamin D3 Deficiency." *Scientific Reports* 7: 14142.

Overview of Contaminants

ARSENIC (As); INORGANIC As (iAs)

Sources

Arsenic in its inorganic form occurs naturally in soil and water worldwide and is found in many different types of ores. As is mobilized and released through a variety of human activities, including smelting, use of arsenic-based pesticides, and many other industrial processes. As also occurs naturally in groundwater in many parts of the world, and people can be exposed from naturally occurring As through household use of this water, including drinking, bathing, cooking, and other activities. Naturally occurring As is also used as irrigation water in many parts of the world, particularly for rice, and is therefore measurable in most rice products, especially those from Southeast Asia.

Health outcomes

Exposures to arsenic have been associated with a variety of health outcomes affecting virtually every organ system in the human body. Among the most obvious clinical symptoms are skin rashes and lesions, such as hyperkeratosis and hyperpigmentation, which may lead to skin cancer. Often these rashes begin on the hands and extremities, and a noted delayed effect of acute or chronic exposure may be seen as Mee's lines in nails (for example, horizontal lines). As is a known human carcinogen, with the strongest association seen with skin cancer, followed by bladder and lung cancer. Arsenic is also associated with neurotoxic and neurodevelopmental outcomes, including cognitive deficits in children and peripheral neuropathy. A variety of other health outcomes has been reported, ranging from gastrointestinal to cardiovascular effects. Reported cardiac effects include altered myocardial depolarization (prolonged QT interval and nonspecific ST-segment changes), cardiac arrhythmias, and ischemic heart disease.

TABLE A.1 **Additional information and detailed profiles on arsenic**

SOURCE	DESCRIPTION
ATSDR (US Agency for Toxic Substances and Disease Registry). 2007. "Toxicological Profile for Arsenic." Atlanta: ATSDR.	Toxicological profile, community information, environmental health and medical education; many resources for health professionals
WHO (World Health Organization). 1981. Arsenic (Environmental Health Criteria 18). Geneva: WHO. file:///C:/Users/16507/Desktop/Downloads/9241540788-eng.pdf.	Detailed toxicological profile
EA (Environment Agency). 2009. "Soil Guideline Values for Inorganic Arsenic in Soil." Science Report SC050021/arsenic SGV. Bristol, UK: EA.	Contains toxicological information; describes environmental fate and exposure pathways
A. Gomez-Caminero, P. Howe, M. Hughes, E. Kenyon, D. R. Lewis, M. Moore, J. Ng, A. Aitio, and G. Becking. 2001. *Environmental Health Criteria 224: Arsenic and Arsenic Compounds.* Geneva: World Health Organization.	Data and review to establish the scientific basis for risk assessment of As
NTP (National Toxicology Program). 2016. "Arsenic and Inorganic Arsenic Compounds." In *Report on Carcinogens*, 14th ed. Washington, DC: US Department of Health and Human Services.	US-based assessment of carcinogenicity of As

Source: World Bank compilation.

CADMIUM (Cd)

Sources

Cadmium occurs naturally at low concentrations in zinc, lead, and copper ores. The primary sources of Cd in the environment include nonferrous metal mining and refining, manufacture and application of phosphate fertilizers, fossil fuel combustion, and waste incineration and disposal. The general population can be exposed primarily through food ingestion, and smokers are exposed to high levels of Cd.

Health outcomes

Sensitive targets of Cd toxicity include the kidneys and bones following oral exposures. The earliest indication of kidney damage in humans is an increased urinary excretion of low-molecular-weight proteins, particularly β2-microglobulin, α1-microglobulin, and retinol binding protein. Increased urinary levels of intracellular enzymes such as N-acetyl-β-glucosaminidase (NAG) and increased excretion of calcium and metallothionein are also early indicators of Cd toxicity. At higher exposure levels, decreases in glomerular filtration rate associated with renal disease have been observed. Prolonged inhalation or ingestion exposure of humans to cadmium at levels leading to renal dysfunction have also been associated with bone disease in individuals with risk factors such as poor nutrition.

TABLE A.2 **Additional information and detailed profiles on cadmium**

SOURCE	DESCRIPTION
ATSDR (US Agency for Toxic Substances and Disease Registry). 2015. "Toxicological Profile for Cadmium." Atlanta: ATSDR.	Detailed toxicological profile, including sampling methods, exposure
ATSDR (US Agency for Toxic Substances and Disease Registry). 2013. "Environmental Health and Medicine Education, Cadmium Toxicity." Atlanta: ATSDR.	Continuing medical education course on cadmium toxicity
Health Canada. "Cadmium."	Health Canada supporting document for drinking water guideline development
WHO (World Health Organization). 2010. "Exposure to Cadmium: A Major Public Health Concern." Geneva: WHO.	World Health Organization detailed supporting toxicological information
IPCS (International Programme on Chemical Safety). 1992. "Environmental Health Criteria 134: Cadmium." Geneva: WHO.	Health criteria document containing detailed toxicological review
Martin, Ian, Hannah Morgan, and Elizabeth Waterfall. 2009. "Soil Guideline Values for Cadmium in Soil." Bristol: UK Environment Agency.	Soil Guideline Values for cadmium in soil
World Bank Group, United Nations Environment Programme, and United Nations Industrial Development Organization. 1999. *Pollution Prevention and Abatement Handbook 1998: Toward Cleaner Production.* Washington, DC: World Bank.	Pollution Prevention and Abatement Handbook, Cd chapter, p. 212

Source: World Bank compilation.

LEAD (Pb)

Sources

Lead occurs naturally in the environment in ores and has many uses, including automobile batteries, leaded gasoline (at one time), lead alloys, use in soldering materials, shielding for X-ray machines, in the manufacture of corrosion-resistant and acid-resistant materials used in the building industry, and a variety of dyes and pigments. Prior to World War II, Pb was used extensively in pesticides. The amount of Pb contained in pipes and plumbing fittings has decreased substantially, but many areas still have public water-distribution systems containing Pb. Other sources of Pb exposure include lead glazing on pottery. Pb has also been found as an additive in nonpharmaceutical health remedies and spices.

Health outcomes

The primary health outcome associated with exposure to Pb is cognitive deficits in children exposed prenatally and throughout childhood.

Pb alters the hematological system by inhibiting the activities of several enzymes involved in heme biosynthesis, particularly δ-aminolevulinic acid dehydratase (ALAD), leading to clinical anemia. Population studies suggest an association between bone-lead levels (measured by XRF) and elevated blood pressure, which may lead to other cardiovascular-health outcomes. Pb is also associated with renal effects, including kidney function, such as glomerular-filtration rate.

TABLE A.3 Additional information and detailed profiles on lead

SOURCE	DESCRIPTION
ATSDR (US Agency for Toxic Substances and Disease Registry). 2020. "Toxicological Profile for Lead." Atlanta: ATSDR.	Toxicological profile, community information, environmental health and medical education; many resources for health professionals
Health Canada. 2013. *Final Human Health State of the Science Report on Lead*. Ottawa: Health Canada.	Toxicological profile, Canadian regulatory perspective
IPCS (International Programme on Chemical Safety). 1995. "Inorganic Lead. Environmental Health Criteria 165." EHC document. Geneva: IPCS, World Health Organization, and United Nations Environment Programme.	Detailed toxicological profile
Nawrot, T. S., L. Thijs, E. M. Den Hond, H. A. Roels, and J. A. Staessen. 2002. "An Epidemiological Re-Appraisal of the Association between Blood Pressure and Blood Lead: A Meta-Analysis." *Journal of Human Hypertension* 16: 123–31.	Meta-analysis of potential cardiovascular effects

Source: World Bank compilation.

Guidelines for Designing and Conducting Home Surveys

A home survey questionnaire will be used to obtain information on relevant demographics, housing characteristics, behaviors, activity patterns, intake rates, other site- or population-specific exposure factors, and basic health information from participants at used lead-acid battery (ULAB) sites. This appendix provides general guidelines for the types of questions that should be included in the household survey and recommended response categories. Important factors that will need to be considered on a site-by-site basis are also noted. The final (formatted) survey questionnaire to be administered in the field should be developed by the in-field research team based on the resources provided here. It is recommended that the questionnaire responses be entered into a portable computer in real time, if possible, to avoid hard-copy losses or subsequent data-entry errors and to facilitate the data-analysis process. It is essential that the household survey be administered to the same individual household members for whom the environmental (chapter 4), biomonitoring (chapter 5), and health-outcome (chapter 6) data are collected. The same home survey instrument should be administered to households in both the identified ULAB sites and matched control sites. Note that any necessary ethical clearances will need to be obtained prior to sample collection by the in-field research team.

GUIDANCE FOR POWER CALCULATIONS, OPTIMAL SAMPLE SIZES, AND HEALTH SURVEY DESIGN

Aday, L. A., and L. J. Cornelius. 2006. *Designing and Conducting Health Surveys: A Comprehensive Guide*, 3rd ed. San Francisco: Jossey-Bass, an imprint of John Wiley & Sons.

This reference is a key resource for designing and conducting health surveys, providing details for designing health surveys using high-quality, effective, and efficient statistical and methodological practices as well as providing optimal sample designs. It is also important that subsequent applications of estimation strategies to the survey data, as well as analytical techniques and interpretations of resultant research findings, are guided by well-grounded statistical theory, and this reference provides these details.

Adcock, C. J. 1997. "Sample Size Determination: A Review." *Journal of the Royal Statistical Society: Series D (The Statistician)* 46 (2): 261–83.

This article provides a review of estimating appropriate sample sizes using both frequentist and Bayesian methods.

Greenland, S. 1993. "Methods for Epidemiologic Analyses of Multiple Exposures: A Review and Comparative Study of Maximum-Likelihood, Preliminary-Testing, and Empirical-Bayes Regression." *Statistics in Medicine* 12 (8): 717–36.

Many epidemiologic investigations are designed to study the effects of multiple exposures. Most of these studies are analyzed either by fitting a risk-regression model with all exposures forced in the model, or by using a preliminary-testing algorithm, such as stepwise regression, to produce a smaller model. Research indicates that hierarchical-modeling methods can outperform these conventional approaches, as discussed in this review.

Lubin, J. H., M. H. Gail, and A. G. Ershow. 1988. "Sample Size and Power for Case-Control Studies When Exposures Are Continuous." *Statistics in Medicine* 7 (3): 363–76.

Environmental exposures are continuous, and dichotomization may result in a "not exposed" category that has little practical meaning. In addition, if risks vary monotonically with exposure, then dichotomization will obscure risk effects and require a greater number of subjects to detect differences in the exposure distributions among cases and referents. Starting from the usual score statistic to detect differences in exposure, this paper develops sample-size formulae for case-control studies with arbitrary exposure distributions; this includes both continuous and dichotomous exposure measurements as special cases.

Lui, K.-J. 1993. "Sample Size Determination for Multiple Continuous Risk Factors in Case-Control Studies." *Biometrics* 49 (3): 873–76.

For a desired power of detecting the association between a disease and several potential risk factors in case-control studies, it is difficult to choose appropriate values for each parameter in the alternative hypothesis. A proposed statistical strategy is discussed.

Lwanga, Stephen Kaggwa, Stanley Lemeshow, and World Health Organization. 1991. *Sample Size Determination in Health Studies: A Practical Manual.* Geneva: World Health Organization. https://apps.who.int/iris/handle/10665/40062

This manual provides the practical and statistical information needed to help investigators decide how large a sample to select from a population targeted for a health study or survey. Designed to perform a "cookbook function," the book uses explanatory text and abundant tabular calculations to vastly simplify the task of determining the minimum sample size needed to obtain statistically valid results given a set of simple hypotheses.

Thomas, D. C., J. Siemiatycki, R. Dewar, J. Robins, M. Goldberg, and B. G. Armstrong. 1985. "The Problem of Multiple Inference in Studies Designed to Generate Hypotheses." *American Journal of Epidemiology* 122 (6): 1080–95.

Epidemiologic research often involves the simultaneous assessment of associations between many risk factors and several disease outcomes. In such situations, often designed to generate hypotheses, multiple univariate hypothesis testing is not an appropriate basis for inference. This paper discusses an approach in which all associations in the data are reported, whether significant or not, followed by a ranking in order of priority for investigation using empirical Bayesian techniques.

EXPOSURE HISTORY RESOURCES

The US Agency for Toxic Substances and Disease Registry (ATSDR) provides educational and resource materials for taking exposure histories in adults and children, and shows how this information can be linked to potential health outcomes.

ANNOTATED REFERENCES ON FOOD FREQUENCY QUESTIONNAIRES

Several food-frequency questionnaire (FFQ) templates are available to use as guides for developing a specific FFQ in the context of exposures in low- and middle-income countries (LMICs). For the research proposed here, an important aspect of the FFQ is to identify the amount and frequency of consumption of locally produced agricultural products and locally caught fish and shellfish that may be affected by contaminants of concern (CoCs) originating from ULAB activities.

The US National Cancer Institute (US NCI) has developed guidance on FFQs to support assessments of dietary and nutritional supplement intake.

The Women's Health Initiative (WHI) is a long-term national health study with both observational and clinical components involving over 40 health centers. The original WHI study included 161,808 postmenopausal women enrolled between 1993 and 1998. The Fred Hutchinson Cancer Research Center in Seattle serves as the WHI Clinical Coordinating Center for data collection, management, and analysis of the WHI. One aspect of the WHI involves application of a detailed dietary assessment including several food-frequency questionnaires.

WHO, UNEP, and IOMC (World Health Organization, United Nations Environment Programme, and Inter-Organization Programme for the Sound Management of Chemicals). 2008. "Guidance for Identifying Populations at Risk from Mercury Exposure." Reference document. Geneva: WHO and UNEP. https://www.who.int/foodsafety/publications/chem/mercuryexposure.pdf.

This publication contains examples of an FFQ, health-assessment questionnaire, and socioeconomic questionnaire, as well as sample collection guidelines for urine, blood, and hair.

ADDITIONAL FFQ REFERENCES

Boynton, P. M., and T. Greenhalgh. "Hands-On Guide to Questionnaire Research: Selecting, Designing, and Developing Your Questionnaire." *BMJ* 328 (7451): 1312–15.

Cade, J., R. Thompson, V. Burley, and D. Warm. 2002. "Development, Validation and Utilisation of Food-Frequency Questionnaires—A Review." *Public Health Nutrition* 5 (4): 567–87.

Matthys, C., I. Pynaert, W. De Keyzer, and S. De Henauw. 2007. "Validity and Reproducibility of an Adolescent Web-Based Food Frequency Questionnaire." *Journal of the American Dietetic Association* 107 (4): 605–10.

Shim, J.-S., K. Oh, and H. C. Kim. 2014. "Dietary Assessment Methods in Epidemiologic Studies." *Epidemiology and Health* 36: e2014009.

ADDITIONAL LMIC-SPECIFIC RESOURCES

Population-based surveys, repeated approximately every five years, are now available for more than 100 LMICs, providing information on nutritional status, health-related behaviors, morbidity, and mortality. These include Demographic and Health Surveys under the auspices of the US Agency for International Development (USAID) and Multiple Indicator Cluster Surveys conducted by the United Nations Children's Fund (UNICEF).

SAMPLE HOME SURVEY QUESTIONNAIRE

Each survey question should have a predetermined list of responses (that is, check-box categories) to ensure uniformity in response options across participants. Open-ended questions should generally be avoided. Note that an adult will need to provide the answer for some (or all) questions on behalf of sampled children.

1. Demographics (provide information on age, sex, length of residence, education, income, household size, and composition)
    1.1 How old are you? (check box for category of age ranges; for example, 6–10 years, 11–15 years)
    1.2 What is your gender identity? (check box)
    1.3 How long have you lived here? (check box for date ranges; for example, 1–2 years, 3–5 years)
    1.4 Where did you live previously? (used to determine whether previous residence was in a similar exposure zone) (*need to determine list of possible neighborhoods, cities, regions in advance)
    1.5 How long did you live there? (check box for date ranges; for example, 1–2 years, 3–5 years)
    1.6 What is your highest level of education? (check box for education ranges; for example, grade school, secondary school)
    1.7 What is your income level? (check box for income ranges) (*need to determine appropriate ranges and $ units in advance)
    1.8 What is the size of your current household? (check box for household ranges; for example, 1–2 people, 3–4 people)
    1.9 Who (and how many) are the other family members? (check all that apply, for example, brother [#], sister [#], mother, father, grandmother)
2. Occupation/School (seeking information on possible workplace, off-site, or take-home exposures)
    2.1 Do you work or attend school outside the home? [if y → 2.2; if n → 3]
    2.2 What do you do? (*need to determine possible industry sectors or schools in advance)
    2.3 Where is that located? (*need to identify possible zone or sector relative to exposure source in advance; map-based)
    2.4 How long have you worked / attended school there? (check box for date ranges)
    2.5 How much time do you spend at your occupation?
    2.6 Do you work with or handle chemicals in any way? [If y → 2.6a; if n → 2.7] (define "chemicals" in advance)

2.6a What chemicals do you work with or handle? (*need to identify possible list of chemicals or materials/products that contain chemicals in advance)

2.6b Do you wear protective equipment? (*need to define personal protective equipment and give list of options; for example, gloves, clothing, dust mask, respirator)

2.6c Do you get any of the chemicals on your skin, hair, or clothing?

2.6d Do you wash off before coming home?

2.6e Do you wash off when you get home or remove clothes?

2.6f Who washes clothing? (check box for possible options; for example, self, spouse, child)

2.6g Where are clothes washed? (*need to identify possible option in advance)

2.7 If attend school, do you play outdoors or in soil? (check box for either/both) [if y → 2.7a; if n → 3.0]

2.7a How often? (check box for frequency ranges; for example, 1–2 days per week, 3–4 days per week)

2.7b How long? (check box for duration ranges; for example, 0.5–1 hour/ day, 2–3 hours/day)

3. Time-Activity Patterns and Lifestyle/Housing Characteristics (seeking information on exposure factors and lifestyle/housing details, including other possible sources of exposure)

3.1 Is there a wood-burning stove and/or fireplace in the home? [if y → 3.1a if n → 3.2]

3.1a What type of wood (or other material) is burned?

3.1b How often?

3.1c Where (for example, kitchen)?

3.2 How close is the home to the road/traffic? (check box for distance ranges; for example, 10–100 yards)

3.3 What kind of traffic (car, bike, horse, foot)? Is the road dusty?

3.4 Do you use pesticides or chemicals inside or outside the home (for example, pest control, gardening, and so forth)? [if y → 3.4.a; if n → 3.5]

3.4a What kinds of chemicals/pesticides do you use? (checkoff list)

3.4b How much do you use? (quantity choices)

3.5 How much time do you spend
- Outside the home (for example, work, school, other activities) (check boxes for time spent at each location; for example, 0.5–1 hour/day) (*Need questions re: whether [how often/how long] spend time playing in soil at home [yard, garden] or other locations)
- Inside the home (approximate time in areas of the home [for example, communal space, kitchen, sleeping, and so forth])

Do you have a dirt floor? [if y → 3.5.a; if n → 3.6]

3.5a How do you (or other family member) clean the floor? (check all cleaning options that apply; for example, sweeping, mopping—may need to identify options in advance)

3.5b How often do you (or other family member) clean the floor? (check box for frequency options; for example, 1–2 times per week, 3–4 times per week)

3.6 What is the floor material? (*need to identify possible materials in advance)

3.7 What is the building material of the home? (*need to identify possible materials in advance)

3.8 What type of roof? (*need to identify possible materials in advance)

3.9 Are there windows? How many? Which rooms? Covered or open? (some findings may be based on personal observations while administering survey)

3.10 How many doors? What material? Gaps around door frame? (some findings may be based on personal observations while administering survey)

3.11 What is ventilation/air exchange like in the home? (*need to identify possible descriptors in advance; may also be based on personal observations)

3.12 Is the home dusty? (questions plus observation) How often cleaned? How cleaned?

3.13 How many floors is home (single versus multistory)?
How is house arranged—bedrooms, kitchen, living area, and so forth (draw map?)

3.14 Do any animals stay inside home? What kind? How many? Where? Contact with household members?

3.15 Do you wear shoes? Track dirt in home?

3.16 Ask questions related to frequency and duration of hand-to-mouth and object-to-mouth activities

3.17 Ask questions related to showering/bathing—where done? Source of water? Frequency and duration?

3.18 Ask questions related to aluminum cookware (contains lead)

4. Health Status (seeking information on current health and possible comorbidities; note this chapter may be superseded in the event of a more formal medical examination—see chapter 6)

4.1 Do you have any diagnosed chronic illnesses? (diabetes, cancer, list and check off with a write-in option?)

4.2 Do you have any acute or chronic health issues? (for example, persistent cough, tremors, skin rashes, and so forth; develop a master list and check off symptoms as appropriate)

4.3 Do you smoke? [If y → 4.3a; if n → 4.4]

4.3a How many cigarettes (or cigars?) do you smoke in a day?

4.3b How long have you been smoking (for example, years)?

4.3c What brand cigarettes? Filtered or unfiltered?

4.4 Do you drink alcohol? [if y → 4.4.a; if n → 4.5]

4.4a How much alcohol do you drink in a typical week?

4.5 Are you physically active?

4.6 Height (cm)

4.7 Weight (kg)

4.8 Body mass index (calculated)

4.9 Ask questions related to malaria, dengue fever, diarrhea, or other region-specific infectious or other issues

4.10 Ask questions (here or below) that get at nutritional or vitamin-deficiency issues

4.11 Use of traditional medicines (contain metals)
Unique to ULAB neurological checklist:

4.12 Do you work at any ULAB-related activities?

4.13 Do you ever experience a metallic taste in your mouth?

4.14 Do you ever have excessive salivation?

4.15 Do you have tremors or do your hands shake?

4.16 Do you have trouble falling or staying asleep?

5. Dietary Information (seeking information on intake rates)

    5.1 In general, how would you describe your diet?

    5.2 Do you eat vegetables/meat/dairy from your own or nearby gardens?

    5.3 Have you eaten seafood in the last 72 hours (important for biomonitoring of As)

    5.4 How much water do you drink in a day? (liters)

    5.5 Where does your water come from? (location, well, tap)

    5.6 Questions related to local fishing, such as types of fish, and so forth FFQ? YES—need questions related to food intake (amount and frequency per day or week)

6. Cost of Illness Economics-Related Information (all questions are based on the previous year)

    6.1 How many days during the last year have you missed work because of illness?

    6.2 How much income did you lose in the last year because of illness?

    6.3 How many times did you visit the emergency room or health center?

    6.4 How many nights did you spend in a hospital or health center?

    6.5 How much did you spend on health care in the last year?

APPENDIX C

Key References and Resource Guides for Environmental Sampling

GUIDELINES FOR SITE CHARACTERIZATION AND DEVELOPING SAMPLING PLANS

When developing a site-specific characterization and sampling plan, multiple resources are available for consultation, as listed and described in table C.1.

TABLE C.1 **Site-characterization resources**

SOURCE	DESCRIPTION
Canadian Council of Ministers of the Environment. *Guidance Manual for Environmental Site Characterization in Support of Environmental and Human Health Risk Assessment.* https://ccme.ca/en/res /guidancemanual-environmentalsitecharacterization_vol _1e.pdf.	Guidance for site characterization, risk assessment, and general contaminated-site assessment
Demetriades, A., and M. Birke. 2015. *Urban Geochemical Mapping Manual: Sampling, Sample Preparation, Laboratory Analysis, Quality Control Check, Statistical Processing and Map Plotting.* Brussels: EuroGeoSurveys.	Guidelines provided by EuroGeoSurveys out of Brussels; provides detailed information on mapping and site characterization from a European perspective
ESDAC (European Soil Data Centre) website: https://esdac .jrc.ec.europa.eu/.	The European Soil Data Centre (ESDAC) of the European Commission's Joint Research Centre is the thematic center for soil-related data in Europe. The goal is to be the single reference point for and to host all relevant soil data and information at the European level. It contains a number of resources: datasets, services or applications, maps, documents, events, projects, and external links.
EPA (US Environmental Protection Agency). 1989. "Interim Final RCRA Facility Investigation (RFI) Guidance, Volume II of IV: Soil, Ground Water and Subsurface Gas Releases." EPA 530/SW-89-031. Washington, DC: EPA.	Provides guidance on site characterization and sampling strategies
EPA (US Environmental Protection Agency). 2014. "Sampling and Analysis Plan—Guidance and Template: Version 4, General Projects." R9QA/009.1. Washington, DC: EPA.	This Sampling and Analysis Plan (SAP) guidance and template is intended to assist organizations in documenting procedural and analytical requirements for projects involving the collection of water, soil, sediment, or other samples taken to characterize areas of potential environmental contamination.

continued

TABLE C.1, *continued*

SOURCE	DESCRIPTION
ISO (International Organization for Standardization). 2017. ISO 18400-105:2017, Soil quality—Sampling—Part 105: Packaging, transport, storage and preservation of samples.	Establishes general principles for packing, preservation, transport, and delivery of soil samples and related materials; requirements for chemical analysis of samples
Olusola, O. I., and O. K. Aisha. 2007. "Towards Standardization of Sampling Methodology for Evaluation of Soil Pollution in Nigeria." *Journal of Applied Sciences and Environmental Management* 11 (3): 81–85.	"…Proposes…procedure…for comparable, representative and cost effective, soil sampling; …explores…policy issues regarding standardization of sampling activities and analytical process as it relates to soil pollution in Nigeria" (Olusola and Aisha 2007, 81).

Source: World Bank compilation.

TABLE C.2 Criteria for analytical-method selection

CRITERION[a]	RATIONALE
Gold standard	Method demonstrates contaminant and matrix specificity; widely used in epidemiological studies
Broadly applicable	Applies to more than just one contaminant
Used in LMIC studies	Documented use in the literature
Feasibility	In field versus send to lab and correlation between field and laboratory results
Cost	To be determined
Detection level	Detection level relative to expected concentrations
Capability	Laboratory likely to have calibrated method
Local capability	In consultation with local expertise

Source: World Bank.
Note: a. Criteria given in order of importance. LMIC = low- to middle-income country.

LABORATORY METHODS FOR ENVIRONMENTAL SAMPLING

The US-based ASTM International (https://www.astm.org/) (formerly known as the American Society for Testing and Materials) and the International Standards Organization (ISO, https://www.iso.org/) are the preeminent organizations providing guidelines and standards for collecting and analyzing environmental samples across different matrices. The specific methods chosen to analyze metals in water, soil, dust, agricultural products, fish, and other matrices—such as sludge, fertilizer, and solid waste—will depend on many factors, some of which can be determined *a priori* and some of which will require additional collaboration by the accredited laboratory performing the analyses and the in-field research team. The general criteria for method evaluation are given in table C.2.

Table C.3 provides a nonexhaustive list of resources most often used internationally in selecting analytical methods for contaminated-site assessments. Relevant US Environmental Protection Agency (EPA) laboratory methods for environmental sampling are shown in table C.4.

TABLE C.3 **Sources of analytical guidelines for contaminated-site assessments**

SOURCE	DESCRIPTION
ASTM International website: https://www.astm.org/.	Internationally recognized as the authority on guidance and guidelines for laboratory testing, collecting samples, metals analysis, and many other standards. Available for purchase individually or by subscription by topic.
EA (Environment Agency). 2006. "The Determination of Metals in Solid Environmental Samples: Methods for the Examination of Waters and Associated Materials." Booklet. Bristol, UK: EA.	Guidance from the UK Environment Agency on laboratory methods for metals in solid matrices.
EPA (US Environmental Protection Agency). n.d. "Collection of Methods." Environment Measurements and Modeling, EPA website: https://www.epa.gov/measurements-modeling /collection-methods.	EPA offices and laboratories, and outside organizations, have developed approved methods for measuring contaminant concentrations. Contains extensive links to many laboratory resources and a complete listing of approved methods.
EPA (US Environmental Protection Agency). n.d. "The SW-486 Compendium." https://www.epa.gov/hw-sw846/sw-846 -compendium.	US EPA's SW-846 Compendium provides a complete listing and guidance of all US EPA-approved laboratory methods. Most methods are intended as guidance.
European Union Reference Laboratory for Heavy Metals in Feed and Food (EURL-HM), European Commission. https://www .feedsafety.org/activities/eurl/eurl-heavy-metals/	Determination of As, Cd, Hg, and Pb in food and feed products including pet food; validated a method for the determination of MeHg in seafood; determination of iAs in food of vegetable origin.
Hageman, P. L. 2007. "Determination of Mercury in Aqueous and Geologic Materials by Continuous Flow–Cold Vapor–Atomic Fluorescence Spectrometry (CVAFS)." In *U.S. Geological Survey Techniques and Methods*, Book 5, Chapter 2. Reston, VA: United States Geological Survey.	Discussion of updated CVAAS methods for determining total Hg in geologic materials and dissolved Hg in aqueous samples; replaces the methods in use prior to 2006.
ISO (International Organization for Standardization). 2013. ISO 16729:2013, Soil quality—Digestion of nitric acid soluble fractions of elements.	Microwave digestion of sludge, treated biowaste, and soil using nitric acid suitable for all metals.
ISO (International Organization for Standardization). 2013. ISO/TS 16965:2013, Soil quality—Determination of trace elements using inductively coupled plasma mass spectrometry (ICP-MS).	Specifies a method for determining metals in aqua regia or nitric acid digests or other extraction solutions of sludge, treated biowaste, and soil.

Source: World Bank compilation.

TABLE C.4 **US EPA laboratory methods**

METHOD #	TITLE	TYPE	ANALYTE	TECHNIQUE	MEDIA/MATRIX	DATE
3005A	Acid Digestion of Waters for Total Recoverable or Dissolved Metals for Analysis by FLAA or ICP Spectroscopy. https://www .epa.gov/sites/default/files/2015 -12/documents/3005a.pdf	Sample preparation	Multi-metal screen; As, Pb	Acid digestion	Surface water, groundwater	July 1992
3010A	Acid Digestion of Aqueous Samples and Extracts for Total Metals for Analysis by FLAA or ICP Spectroscopy. https://www .epa.gov/sites/default/files/2015 -12/documents/3010a.pdf	Sample preparation	Multi-metal screen; As, Pb	Acid digestion	Aqueous samples, extracts, wastes with suspended solids	July 1992
3015A	Microwave Assisted Acid Digestion of Aqueous Samples and Extracts. https://www.epa .gov/sites/default/files/2015-12 /documents/3015a.pdf	Sample preparation	Multi-metal screen; As, Pb	Microwave-assisted acid digestion	Aqueous samples, drinking water, extracts, wastes with suspended solids	Feb. 2007

continued

TABLE C.4, *continued*

METHOD #	TITLE	TYPE	ANALYTE	TECHNIQUE	MEDIA/MATRIX	DATE
3020A	Acid Digestion of Aqueous Samples and Extracts for Total Metals for Analysis by GFAA Spectroscopy. https://www.epa.gov/hw-sw846/sw-846-test-method-3020a-acid-digestion-aqueous-samples-and-extracts-total-metals-analysis	Sample preparation	Pb	Acid digestion	Aqueous samples, extracts, wastes with suspended solids	July 1992
3031	Acid Digestion of Oils for Metals Analysis by Atomic Absorption or ICP Spectrometry. https://19january2017snapshot.epa.gov/sites/production/files/2015-07/documents/epa-3031.pdf	Sample preparation	Multi-metal screen; As, Pb	Acid digestion	Oils, oil sludges, tars, waxes, paints, paint sludges, other viscous petroleum products	Dec. 1996
3040A	Dissolution Procedure for Oils, Greases, or Waxes. https://www.epa.gov/sites/default/files/2015-12/documents/3040a.pdf	Sample preparation	Multi-metal screen; As, Pb	Solvent dissolution	Oils, greases, waxes	Dec. 1996
3050B	Acid Digestion of Sediments, Sludges, and Soils. https://www.epa.gov/sites/default/files/2015-06/documents/epa-3050b.pdf	Sample preparation	Multi-metal screen; As, Pb	Acid digestion	Sediments, sludges, soils, and oils	Dec. 1996
3051A	Microwave Assisted Acid Digestion of Sediments, Sludges, Soils, and Oils. https://www.epa.gov/sites/default/files/2015-06/documents/epa-3050b.pdf	Sample preparation	Multi-metal screen; As, Pb	Microwave-assisted acid digestion	Sediments, sludges, soils, and oils	Feb. 2007
7010	Graphite Furnace Atomic Absorption Spectrophotometry. https://www.epa.gov/sites/default/files/2015-07/documents/epa-7010.pdf	Determinative	Multi-metal screen; As, Pb	Graphite furnace atomic absorption spectrophotometry (GFAA or GFAAS)	Groundwater, domestic wastes, industrial wastes, extracts, soils, sludges, sediments	Feb. 2007
7000B	Flame Atomic Absorption Spectrophotometry. https://www.epa.gov/sites/default/files/2015-12/documents/7000b.pdf	Determinative	Pb	Flame atomic absorption spectrophotometry (FLAA or FAAS)	Groundwater, aqueous samples, extracts, industrial waste, soils, sludges, sediments	Feb. 2007
6800	Elemental and Molecular Speciated Isotope Dilution Mass Spectrometry. https://www.epa.gov/sites/default/files/2015-12/documents/6800.pdf	Determinative	Pb	Isotope dilution mass spectrometry (IDMS), molecular speciated isotope dilution mass spectrometry (SIDMS)	Water samples, solid samples, extracts, digests, blood, foods	July 2014

continued

TABLE C.4, *continued*

METHOD #	TITLE	TYPE	ANALYTE	TECHNIQUE	MEDIA/MATRIX	DATE
6200	Field Portable X-Ray Fluorescence Spectrometry for the Determination of Elemental Concentrations in Soil and Sediment. https://www.epa.gov/hw-sw846/sw-846-test-method-6200-field-portable-x-ray-fluorescence-spectrometry-determination	Determinative	Multi-metal screen; As, Pb	X-ray fluorescence	Soils, sediment	Feb. 2007
6020B	Inductively Coupled Plasma-Mass Spectrometry. https://www.epa.gov/sites/default/files/2015-12/documents/6020b.pdf	Determinative	Multi-metal screen; As, Pb	Inductively coupled plasma-mass spectrometry (ICP-MS)	Water samples, waste extracts, digests	July 2014
6010D	Inductively Coupled Plasma-Optical Emissions Spectrometry. https://www.epa.gov/hw-sw846/sw-846-test-method-6010d-inductively-coupled-plasma-optical-emission-spectrometry-icp-oes	Determinative	Multi-metal screen; As, Pb	Inductively coupled plasma-atomic (or optical) emission spectrometry (ICP-AES or ICP-OES)	Groundwater, digested aqueous and solid matrices	July 2014
3052	Microwave Assisted Acid Digestion of Siliceous and Organically Based Matrices. https://19january2017snapshot.epa.gov/hw-sw846/sw-846-test-method-3052-microwave-assisted-acid-digestion-siliceous-and-organically-based_.html	Sample preparation	Multi-metal screen; As, Pb	Microwave-assisted acid digestion	Siliceous matrices, organic matrices, and other complex matrices	Dec. 1996
7472	Mercury in Aqueous Samples and Extracts by Anodic Stripping Voltammetry (ASV). https://www.epa.gov/sites/default/files/2015-12/documents/7472.pdf	Determinative	Hg	Anodic stripping voltammetry (ASV)	Drinking water, natural surface water, seawater, domestic or industrial wastewater, soil extracts	Dec. 1996
7473	Mercury in Solids and Solutions by Thermal Decomposition, Amalgamation, and Atomic Absorption Spectrophotometry. https://www.epa.gov/hw-sw846/sw-846-test-method-7473-mercury-solids-and-solutions-thermal-decomposition-amalgamation-and	Determinative	Hg	Thermal decomposition and atomic absorption spectrophotometry (AAS)	Solids, aqueous samples, digested solutions	Feb. 2007
7474	Mercury in Sediment and Tissue Samples by Atomic Fluorescence Spectrometry. https://www.epa.gov/hw-sw846/sw-846-test-method-7474-mercury-sediment-and-tissue-samples-atomic-fluorescence	Determinative	Hg	Atomic fluorescence spectrometry (AFS)	Sediment, tissue	Feb. 2007

Source: World Bank compilation.
Note: As = arsenic; EPA = US Environmental Protection Agency; FLAA = lead analysis by flame atomic absorption; GFAA = graphite furnace atomic absorption spectroscopy; Hg = mercury; ICP = inductively coupled plasma analysis; Pb = lead.

BIOACCESSIBILITY AND BIOAVAILABILITY OF LEAD AND ARSENIC: US EPA GUIDANCE

EPA (US Environmental Protection Agency). 2007. "Guidance for Evaluating the Oral Bioavailability of Metals in Soils for Use in Human Health Risk Assessment." OSWER 9285.7-80. Washington, DC: EPA.

EPA (US Environmental Protection Agency). 2015. "Guidance for Sample Collection for *In Vitro* Bioaccessibility Assay for Lead (Pb) in Soil." OSWER 9200.3-100. Washington, DC: EPA.

EPA (US Environmental Protection Agency). 2017. "Method 1340: *In Vitro* Bioaccessibility Assay for Lead in Soil." SW-846 Update VI. Washington, DC: EPA.

EPA (US Environmental Protection Agency). 2017. "Release of Standard Operating Procedure for an In Vitro Bioaccessibility Assay for Lead and Arsenic in Soil and 'Validation Assessment of In Vitro Arsenic Bioaccessibility Assay for Predicting Relative Bioavailability of Arsenic in Soils and Soil-like Materials at Superfund Sites.'" OLEM 9355.4-29, April 20. Washington, DC: EPA. https://clu-in.org/download/contaminantfocus/arsenic/arsenic-OLEM-9355.4-29.pdf.

DUST SAMPLE COLLECTION

ASTM International. 2018. "ASTM D6966—18, Standard Practice for Collection of Settled Dust Samples Using Wipe Sampling Methods for Subsequent Determination of Metals." West Conshohocken, PA: ASTM International. https://www.astm.org/Standards/D6966.htm.

ASTM International. 2020. "ASTM E1728—20, Standard Practice for Collection of Settled Dust Samples Using Wipe Sampling Methods for Subsequent Lead Determination." West Conshohocken, PA: ASTM International. https://www.astm.org/Standards/E1728.htm.

EPA (US Environmental Protection Agency). 1966. "Analysis of Composite Wipe Samples for Lead Content." EPA 747-R-96-003. Washington, DC: EPA.

Friederich, N. J., M. Karin, K. M. Bauer, B. D. Schultz, and T. S. Holderman. 1999. "The Use of Composite Dust Wipe Samples as a Means of Assessing Lead Exposure." *American Industrial Hygiene Association Journal* 60 (3): 326–33. doi:10.1080/00028899908984449.

HUD (US Department of Housing and Urban Development). 2012. "Wipe Sampling of Settled Dust for Lead Determination." In *Guidelines for the Evaluation and Control of Lead-Based Paint Hazards in Housing*, 2nd ed., Appendix 13.1. Washington, DC: HUD. https://www.hud.gov/sites/documents/LBPH-40.PDF.

Biomonitoring Resources

Biomonitoring and biological-sample collection should be conducted under the supervision of a trained professional, and most institutional review boards and ethics-review organizations will make that a prerequisite for data collection. This appendix provides links to accepted methods for sample collection across biological matrices, as well as information on efforts worldwide to coordinate biomonitoring programs.

Table D.1 provides an overview of biomonitoring studies conducted in low- and middle-income countries (LMICs).

TABLE D.1 Selected biomonitoring studies for lead and metals with application to LMICs

REFERENCE	LOCATION	INDUSTRY	POLLUTANT	BIOLOGICAL MATRIX	ANALYTICAL METHOD	ANALYTICAL LAB	NOTES
Lead							
Baghurst et al. (1992)	Port Pirie, South Australia	Lead smelter	Lead	Capillary blood	Electrothermal atomization atomic absorption spectrometry	Department of Chemical Pathology at Adelaide Centre for Women's and Children's Health	Cited prior study showing close correlation ($r = 0.97$) b/w capillary and venous sampling (Calder et al. 1986)
Malcoe et al. (2002)	Northeastern Oklahoma	Lead and zinc mining	Lead	Venous blood	Graphite furnace atomic absorption spectrometry	Samples shipped to Oklahoma State Department of Health laboratory	
Jones et al. (2011)	Senegal (Thiaroye Sur Mer)	Lead-acid battery disposal	Lead	(1) Venous blood (2) Capillary blood	(1) Graphite furnace atomic absorption spectrometry (2) LeadCare portable test kits	(1) Samples shipped to Pasteur Cerba-certified lab (France) (2) In field	"HI" LeadCare readings sent to lab

continued

TABLE D.1, *continued*

REFERENCE	LOCATION	INDUSTRY	POLLUTANT	BIOLOGICAL MATRIX	ANALYTICAL METHOD	ANALYTICAL LAB	NOTES
Lo et al. (2012)	Zamfara State, Nigeria	Gold-ore processing	Lead	Venous blood	LeadCare II portable analyzer	Samples were analyzed at the Blood Lead and Inorganic Metals Lab (Gusau, Zamfara)	Product lots of all blood collection supplies were prescreened for lead contamination by CDC labs, and supplies were stored in plastic bags before collection to prevent in-field contamination
Caravanos et al. (2014)	Kabwe, Zambia	Lead mining and smelting	Lead	Capillary blood	LeadCare II portable analyzer	In field	
Gao et al. (2001)	Wuxi City, China	n.a.	Lead	Capillary blood	Graphite furnace atomic absorption spectrometry	Shipped to School of Public Health, Beijing Medical University	
Riddell et al. (2007); Solon et al. (2008)	Central Philippines	n.a.	Lead	Venous blood	LeadCare analyzer; subset analyzed using atomic absorption spectroscopy	Samples were analyzed at a central laboratory in Manila	Cited previous field work demonstrating good correlation ($r = 0.829$) between LeadCare device and atomic absorption spectrometry (Counter et al. 1998); study also measured hemoglobin (HemoCue Blood Hemoglobin Photometer) and red blood cell folate (Architect system)
Xie et al. (2013)	China (16 cities)	n.a.	Lead	Capillary blood	BH2100 tungsten atomizer absorption spectrophotometer	n.a.	QA/QC program for blood lead levels higher than 10 ug/dL (used double test method)
Daniell et al. (2015)	Hung Yen Province, northern Vietnam	Battery recycling	Lead	Capillary blood	LeadCare II portable analyzer	In field	Children only; confirmatory venous sampling for high field levels; extensive soil, survey, medical data also collected
Grigoryan et al. (2016)	Northern Armenia	Metal mining and smelting	Lead	Capillary blood	LeadCare II portable analyzer	In field	Blood samples collected following CDC recommended finger-stick method; cites results of CLIA waiver clinical field trials that found good correlation ($r = 0.979$) between this device and graphite furnace atomic absorption spectrometry (GFAAS)

continued

TABLE D.1, *continued*

REFERENCE	LOCATION	INDUSTRY	POLLUTANT	BIOLOGICAL MATRIX	ANALYTICAL METHOD	ANALYTICAL LAB	NOTES
Metals							
Were et al. (2008)	Nairobi, Kenya	School-age children in industrial areas	Lead, cadmium, calcium, zinc, and iron	Fingernails	Atomic absorption spectrometer with acid digestion	Kenyatta University Research Laboratory and Mines and Geology Analytical Research Department, Nairobi	
Qu et al. (2012)	Jiangsu Province, China	Lead-zinc mining	Metals	Hair	Inductively coupled argon plasma mass spectrometry (USEPA 6020A) for metals Thermal decomposition, amalgamation, and atomic absorption spectrophotometry (USEPA 7473) for Hg	—	Ag, Cd, Cr, Cu, Ni, Pb, Se, Ti, Zn, Hg; notes that hair useful for assessing long-term exposure and for certain metals (Pb, Hg) but not others (Zn, Cu, Cd)
Thakur et al. (2010)	Punjab, India	Wastewater drains	Metals, pesticides	Blood Urine Human milk	Community-based interviews of women and children; clinical examination and records review by medical doctors of selected cases.	—	Urine (Hg, Cd, Pb, As, Se) Blood/milk (pesticides)
Röllin et al. (2009)	South Africa	Multiple (for example, industrial and mining sites)	Metals	Venous blood (before delivery) Umbilical cord blood	Element 2 mass spectrometer	Samples shipped to University of Tromso, Norway, and analyzed at National Institute for Occupational Health	Cd, Hg, Pb, Mn, CO, Cu, Zn, As, Se
Banza et al. (2009)	Congo, Dem. Rep.	Metal mining and smelting	Metals	Urine (spot)	Inductively coupled argon plasma mass spectrometry	Samples analyzed in Laboratory of Industrial Toxicology and Occupational Medicine Unit (Belgium)	Al, Sb, As, Cd, Cr, Co, Cu, Pb, Mn, Mo, Ni, Se, Te, Sn, U, V, Zn; creatinine adjusted
Ibeto and Okoye (2010)	Enugu State, Nigeria	n.a.	Metals	Venous blood	GBC atomic absorption spectrophotometer	University of Nigeria Nsukka, Enugu State	Ni, Mn, Cr
Alatise and Schrauzer (2010)	Nigeria, Africa	n.a.	Metals	Blood (fasting) Hair (scalp) Breast biopsy	Inductively coupled plasma mass spectrometry	—	Cu, Zn, Pb, Se, Cd, Hg, As, Mn, Sr, Ca, Mg, Li, Co, Zn/Cu, Ca/Mg; notes various interactions (for example, Pb interacts with Se and iodine in vivo)

continued

TABLE D.1, *continued*

REFERENCE	LOCATION	INDUSTRY	POLLUTANT	BIOLOGICAL MATRIX	ANALYTICAL METHOD	ANALYTICAL LAB	NOTES
Caravanos et al. (2013)	Ghana, West Africa	E-waste dumping and recycling	Metals	Urine (first void) Venous blood (serum)	Graphite furnace atomic absorption spectrometry; whole blood spun to isolate cells to produce serum	Ghana Standards Board Forensic Lab in Accra	Ba, Cd, Co, Mn, Cr, Cu, Fe, Hg, Pb, Se, Zn; Sample collection equipment and containers were prescreened or soaked in trace metal-grade nitric acid; analytical flaw in using blood serum because lead resides in erythrocyte
Obiri et al. (2016)	Tarkwa Nsuaem Municipality and the Prestea Huni Valley District, Ghana	Mining	Metals	Whole blood Venous blood (serum)	Neutron activation analysis	Ghana Atomic Energy Commission	As, Cd, Hg, Cu, Pb, Zn, Mn; also administered a health questionnaire. Fasting sample
Sanders et al. (2014)	Red River Delta, Vietnam	Smelting (automobile batteries)	Metals	Capillary blood Toenail	LeadCare II portable analyzer Toenails extracted using modified Method 3050B	In-field toenail samples shipped to RTI International (Research Triangle Park, NC)	In whole blood and serum
Jasso-Pineda et al. (2007)	Villa de la Paz, Mexico	Mining	Metals	Venous blood Urine (first void)	Atomic absorption spectrometry	Universidad Autónoma de San Luis Potosí, Mexico	Blood (lead) Urine (spot)
Uriah et al. (2013)	Zamfara State, Nigeria	Artisanal gold mining	Lead, mercury				

Source: World Bank compilation.

Note: Bibliographic information for references is listed below by topic. n.a. = not applicable. Al = aluminum; As = arsenic; Ba = barium; Ca = calcium; Cd = cadmium; Co = cobalt; Cr = chromium; Cu = copper; Fe = iron; Hg = mercury; Li = lithium; MeHg = methylmercury; Mg = magnesium; Mn = manganese; Mo = molybdenum; Ni = nickel; Pb = lead; Sb = antimony; Se = Selenium; Sn = tin; Sr = strontium; Te = tellurium; Ti = titanium; U = uranium; V = vanadium; Zn = zinc.

SAMPLE-COLLECTION GUIDELINES FOR TRACE ELEMENTS IN BLOOD AND URINE

APHL (Association of Public Health Laboratories). n.d. "Biomonitoring" online resource page includes the National Biomonitoring Network (NBN) of federal, regional, state, and local laboratories that conduct biomonitoring for use in public health practice. APHL, Silver Spring, MD. https://www.aphl.org/programs/environmental_health/nbn/Pages/default.aspx.

ATSDR (US Agency for Toxic Substances and Disease Registry). 2020. "Analytical Methods." Discussion of measuring lead in biological matrices in chapter 7 of "Toxicological Profile for Lead," ATSDR, Atlanta. https://www.ncbi.nlm.nih.gov/books/NBK158761/.

CDC (US Centers for Disease Control and Prevention). 2006. "CDC Specimen-Collection Protocol for a Chemical-Exposure Event." Infographic, CDC, Atlanta. https://www.health.ny.gov/guidance/oph/wadsworth/chemspecimencollection.pdf.

CDC (US Centers for Disease Control and Prevention). 2013. "Guidelines for Measuring Lead in Blood Using Point of Care Instruments." Guidance from the Advisory Committee on Childhood Lead Poisoning Prevention of the CDC, Atlanta. https://www.cdc.gov/nceh/lead/acclpp/20131024_pocguidelines_final.pdf.

CLSI (Clinical Laboratory Standards Institute). 2013. *Measurement Procedures for the Determination of Lead Concentrations in Blood and Urine, 2nd Ed.* CLSI document C40-A2. Wayne, PA: CLSI. https://clsi.org/standards/products/clinical-chemistry-and-toxicology/documents/c40/.

Cornelis, R., B. Heinzow, R. F. M. Herber, J. M. Christensen, O. M. Poulsen, E. Sabbioni, D. M. Templeton, Y. Thomassen, M. Vahter, and O. Vesterberg. 1995. "Sample Collection Guidelines for Trace Elements in Blood and Urine." *Pure and Applied Chemistry* 67 (8–9): 1575–1608. http://publications.iupac.org/pac-2007/1995/pdf/6708x1575.pdf.

Cornelis, R., B. Heinzow, R. F. M. Herber, J. M. Christensen, O. M. Poulsen, E. Sabbioni, D. M. Templeton, Y. Thomassen, M. Vahter, and O. Vesterberg. 1996. "Sample Collection Guidelines for Trace Elements in Blood and Urine." *Journal of Trace Elements in Medicine and Biology* 10 (2): 103–27.

EPA (US Environmental Protection Agency). 2019. "Guidelines for Human Exposure Assessment." EPA/100/B-19/001, Risk Assessment Forum. Washington, DC: EPA. https://www.epa.gov/sites/default/files/2020-01/documents/guidelines_for_human_exposure_assessment_final2019.pdf.

FDA and NIH (US Food and Drug Administration and National Institutes of Health). 2016. "BEST (Biomarkers, EndpointS, and other Tools) Resource." Glossary copublished by the FDA, Silver Spring, MD; and NIH, Bethesda, MD. https://www.ncbi.nlm.nih.gov/books/NBK326791/pdf/Bookshelf_NBK326791.pdf.

Heppner, Claudia. 2011. "Biomarkers in Risk Assessment: Application for Chemical Contaminants." PowerPoint presentation at the EU Decision Makers Meeting, "Use of Human Biomonitoring for Policy Making," Munich, May 4. http://www.eu-hbm.info/cophes/4_Biomarkersinriskassessment.pdf.

IPCS (International Programme on Chemical Safety). 1993. *Biomarkers and Risk Assessment: Concepts and Principles.* Environmental Health Criteria (EHC) 155. Geneva: World Health Organization. http://apps.who.int/iris/bitstream/handle/10665/39037/9241571551-eng.pdf;jsessionid=77D78AFFF865ABE58A666BB4941A9330?sequence=1.

MEASURE Evaluation. 2000. "Biological and Clinical Data Collection in Population Surveys in Less Developed Countries." Summary of MEASURE Evaluation meeting, National Academy of Sciences, Washington, DC, January 24–25. https://www.who.int/hiv/pub/surveillance/en/biomarkers.pdf?ua=1.

WHO (World Health Organization). 2010. *WHO Guidelines on Drawing Blood: Best Practices in Phlebotomy.* Geneva: WHO. https://www.euro.who.int/__data/assets/pdf_file/0005/268790/WHO-guidelines-on-drawing-blood-best-practices-in-phlebotomy-Eng.pdf.

WHO (World Health Organization). 2011. *Brief Guide to Analytical Methods for Measuring Lead in Blood.* Geneva: WHO. http://www.who.int/ipcs/assessment/public_health/lead_blood.pdf.

Dried blood spots

Crimmins, E. M., J. D. Faul, J. K. Kim, and D. R. Weir. 2017. "Documentation of Blood-Based Biomarkers in the 2014 Health and Retirement Study." Report, Survey Research Center, Institute for Social Research, University of Michigan, Ann Arbor.

Crimmins, E., J. K. Kim, H. McCreath, J. Faul, D. Weir, and T. Seeman. 2014. "Validation of Blood-Based Assays Using Dried Blood Spots for Use in Large Population Studies." *Biodemography and Social Biology* 60 (1): 38–48. doi:10.1080/19485565.2014.901885.

Delahaye, L., B. Janssens, and C. Stove. 2017. "Alternative Sampling Strategies for the Assessment of Biomarkers of Exposure." *Current Opinion in Toxicology* 4: 43–51.

Freeman, J. D., L. M. Rosman, J. D. Ratcliff, P. T. Strickland, D. R. Graham, and E. K. Silbergeld. 2017. "State of the Science in Dried Blood Spots." *Clinical Chemistry* 64 (4): 656–79.

Funk, W. E., J. D. Pleil, D. J. Sauter, T. McDade, and J. L. Holl. 2015. "Use of Dried Blood Spots for Estimating Children's Exposures to Heavy Metals in Epidemiological Research." *Journal of Environmental & Analytical Toxicology* 7 (2): 1–9.

Wagner, M., D. Tonoli, E. Varesio, and G. Hopfgartner. 2016. "The Use of Mass Spectrometry to Analyze Dried Blood Spots." *Mass Spectrometry Reviews* 35 (3): 361–438.

Cardiovascular (C-reactive protein)

Ahn, J. S., S. Choi, S. H. Jang, H. J. Chang, J. H. Kim, K. B. Nahm, S. W. Oh, and E. Y. Choi. 2003. "Development of a Point-of-Care Assay System for High-Sensitivity C-Reactive Protein in Whole Blood." *Clinica Chimica Acta* 332 (1–2): 51–59.

Brindle, E., M. Fujita, J. Shofer, and K. A. O'Connor. 2010. "Serum, Plasma, and Dried Blood Spot High-Sensitivity C-Reactive Protein Enzyme Immunoassay for Population Research." *Journal of Immunological Methods* 362 (1–2): 112–20.

McDade, T. W., J. Burhop, and J. Dohnal. 2004. "High-Sensitivity Enzyme Immunoassay for C-Reactive Protein in Dried Blood Spots." *Clinical Chemistry* 50 (3): 652–54.

Ochoa-Martínez, Á. C., E. D. Cardona-Lozano, L. Carrizales-Yáñez, and I. N. Pérez-Maldonado. 2018. "Serum Concentrations of New Predictive Cardiovascular Disease Biomarkers in Mexican Women Exposed to Lead." *Archives of Environmental Contamination and Toxicology* 74 (2): 248–58.

Peña, M. S. B., and A. Rollins. 2017. "Environmental Exposures and Cardiovascular Disease: A Challenge for Health and Development in Low- and Middle-Income Countries." *Cardiology Clinics* 35 (1): 71–86.

Roberts, W. L., L. Moulton, T. C. Law, G. Farrow, M. Cooper-Anderson, J. Savory, and N. Rifai. 2001. "Evaluation of Nine Automated High-Sensitivity C-Reactive Protein Methods: Implications for Clinical and Epidemiological Applications. Part 2." *Clinical Chemistry* 47 (3): 418–25.

Roberts, W. L., E. L. Schwarz, S. Ayanian, and N. Rifai. 2001, "Performance Characteristics of a Point of Care C-Reactive Protein Assay." *Clinica Chimica Acta* 314 (1–2): 255–59.

Roberts W. L., R. Sedrick, L. Moulton, A. Spencer, and N. Rifai. 2000. "Evaluation of Four Automated High-Sensitivity C-Reactive Protein Methods: Implications for Clinical and Epidemiological Applications." *Clinical Chemistry* 46 (4): 461–68.

Point-of-care (POC) and in-field diagnostic assays and methods

Byrnes, S., G. Thiessen, and E. Fu. 2013. "Progress in the Development of Paper-Based Diagnostics for Low-Resource Point-of-Care Settings." *Bioanalysis* 5 (22): 2821–36.

Drain, P. K., E. P. Hyle, F. Noubary, K. A. Freedberg, D. Wilson, W. R. Bishai, W. Rodriguez, and I. V. Bassett. 2014. "Diagnostic Point-of-Care Tests in Resource-Limited Settings." *Lancet Infectious Diseases* 14 (3): 239–49.

Garcia, P. J., P. You, G. Fridley, D. Mabey, and R. Peeling. 2015. "Point-of-Care Diagnostic Tests for Low-Resource Settings." *Lancet Global Health* 3 (5): e257–8.

Gubala, V., L. F. Harris, A. J. Ricco, M. X .Tan, and D. E. Williams. 2011. "Point of Care Diagnostics: Status and Future." *Analytical Chemistry* 84 (2): 487–515.

Sharma, S., J. Zapatero-Rodríguez, P. Estrela, and R. O'Kennedy. 2015. "Point-of-Care Diagnostics in Low Resource Settings: Present Status and Future Role of Microfluidics." *Biosensors* 5 (3): 577–601.

Shaw, J. L. 2016. "Practical Challenges Related to Point of Care Testing." *Practical Laboratory Medicine* 4: 22–29.

Song, Y., Y. Y. Huang, X. Liu, X. Zhang, M. Ferrari, and L. Qin. 2014. "Point-of-Care Technologies for Molecular Diagnostics Using a Drop of Blood." *Trends in Biotechnology* 32 (3): 132–39.

St. John, A., and C. P. Price. 2014. "Existing and Emerging Technologies for Point-of-Care Testing." *Clinical Biochemist Reviews* 35 (3): 155–67.

Vashist, S. K., P. B. Luppa, L. Y. Yeo, A. Ozcan, and J. H. Luong. 2015. "Emerging Technologies for Next-Generation Point-of-Care Testing." *Trends in Biotechnology* 33 (11): 692–705.

Xu, X., A. Akay, H. Wei, S. Wang, B. Pingguan-Murphy, B. E. Erlandsson, X. Li, et al. 2015. "Advances in Smartphone-Based Point-of-Care Diagnostics." *Proceedings of the IEEE* 103 (2): 236–47.

MODELING TOOLS

A variety of modeling approaches are available for quantifying and predicting contaminant fate, transport, and external and internal exposures from source to outcome as presented in the conceptual site model (CSM). Fate and transport models are used to quantify the movement of contaminants through environmental media to the point of exposure. For example, air-quality models predict wet and dry deposition of airborne contaminants from a variety of sources based on local estimates of wind speed, rainfall, and other parameters. Similarly, groundwater models predict expected concentrations in groundwater from leaching in soils or other mechanisms. These models could be used together with measured soil concentrations (chapter 3) and site-specific parameters to predict groundwater concentrations, which could then be verified using measured groundwater measurements (chapter 3).

There are many different models that could be applied along the continuum from contaminant source to health outcome, and they vary in complexity and required inputs. This appendix provides links to resources to consult in deciding which models to use and identifies a limited set of specific models relevant to assessing exposure to metals in low- and middle-income countries (LMICs). For example, the integrated exposure uptake biokinetic model for lead in children (IEUBK) is a model developed by the US Environmental Protection Agency (EPA) to predict expected blood lead levels in children from measured concentrations in soil. This model, together with LMIC-specific exposure factors (appendix B), could be combined to predict the biomonitoring data (chapter 4). Similarly, several physiologically based pharmacokinetic (PBPK) models exist to link external exposure concentrations (chapter 3) to internal concentrations in target organs, tissues, and blood, which can then be verified in a limited way (for example, blood, urine, hair) using the biomonitoring data (chapter 4). This may allow for less data collection in the future or achieve other goals.

Depending on the model's complexity, some degree of training and experience with specific models is generally required to gain proficiency with their use. Models generally require site-specific calibration and verification to effectively support decision-making.

EPA (US Environmental Protection Agency). 2021. "Integrated Exposure Uptake Biokinetic Model for Lead in Children, Windows® version (IEUBKwin v2) (May 2021) 32/64-bit version." Software, EPA, Washington, DC.

The Integrated Exposure Uptake Biokinetic (IEUBK) Model for Lead in Children is stand-alone, Windows-based software developed by the US EPA. The model predicts the distribution of expected blood lead concentrations for a hypothetical child or population of children based on measured or assumed concentrations of Pb in the environment, particularly soil and drinking water (chapter 3). From this distribution, the model calculates the probability that predicted blood lead concentrations will exceed a user-defined level of concern (default 10 μg/dL). The user can then explore an array of possible changes in exposure media that would reduce the probability that blood lead concentrations would be above this level of concern. Beginning in 1990, the model has undergone many iterations and review cycles, and has been well vetted in the literature and elsewhere.

The model is optimized for children less than seven years old who are exposed to environmental Pb from many sources. The model can also be used to predict cleanup levels for various media assuming residential land use. Studies show the model is most sensitive to the amount of soil and dust ingested per day. In decreasing order of sensitivity, predicted Pb uptake is moderately sensitive to the assumed absorption fraction for soil/dust and diet, the soil Pb concentration, the indoor dust Pb concentration, dietary-lead concentration, contribution of soil lead to indoor dust lead, and the half-saturation absorbable intake (based on output-input ratio). Finally, the predicted probability of exceeding a specified level of concern is highly sensitive to changes in the geometric standard deviation (GSD). The GSD is a measure of the variability among individuals who have contact with a fixed lead concentration and is based on analyses of data from neighborhoods having paired sets of environmental concentration and blood Pb data from high-income countries (HICs). This value likely differs for LMICs.

EPA (US Environmental Protection Agency). n.d. Lead at Superfund Sites: Frequent Questions from Risk Assessors on the Adult Lead Model Methodology. Questions, input variables, and application, EPA, Washington, DC.

While the IEUBK model is designed for children, the Adult Lead Model (ALM) focuses on adults. The required inputs are similar, but the ALM model is designed for adult populations.

Physiologically based pharmacokinetic (PBPK) models for metals

PBPK models are contaminant-specific and typically used to evaluate contaminant disposition in the human body following exposure. The models are generally based on studies in which animals, often rodents, are exposed to known quantities of contaminants via specific exposure routes and the animals are sacrificed at various time points and organ-specific contaminant concentrations assessed. The animal data relate to humans through a comparison of physiological-rate constants (for example, breathing rate, blood volume, and so on).

Kenyon, E. M., and H. J. Clewell III. 2015. "Toxicokinetics and Pharmacokinetic Modeling of Arsenic." In *Arsenic: Exposure Sources, Health Risks, and Mechanisms of Toxicity*, edited by J. C. States, 495–510. Hoboken, NJ: John Wiley & Sons. https://onlinelibrary.wiley.com/doi/book/10.1002/9781118876992.

This book illustrates the chemistry, toxicology, and health effects of As using novel modeling techniques, case studies, experimental data, and future perspectives. Chapter 22 in particular focuses on PBPK modeling for As.

Liao, C. M., T. L. Lin, and S. C. Chen. 2008. "A Weibull-PBPK Model for Assessing Risk of Arsenic-Induced Skin Lesions in Children." *Science of the Total Environment* 392 (2–3): 203–17.

Mumtaz, M., J. Fisher, B. Blount, and P. Ruiz. 2012. "Application of Physiologically Based Pharmacokinetic Models in Chemical Risk Assessment." *Journal of Toxicology*. https://www.ncbi.nlm.nih.gov/pmc/articles/PMC3317240/.

Ruiz, P., B. A. Fowler, J. D. Osterloh, J. Fisher, and M. Mumtaz. 2010. "Physiologically Based Pharmacokinetic (PBPK) Tool Kit for Environmental Pollutants–Metals." *SAR and QSAR in Environmental Research* 21 (7–8): 603–18.

Ruiz, P., M. Ray, J. Fisher, and M. Mumtaz. 2011. "Development of a Human Physiologically Based Pharmacokinetic (PBPK) Toolkit for Environmental Pollutants." *International Journal of Molecular Sciences* 12 (11): 7469–80.

Bioaccumulation models

Alatise, Olusegun I., and Gerhard N. Schrauzer. 2010. "Lead Exposure: A Contributing Cause of the Current Breast Cancer Epidemic in Nigerian Women." *Biological Trace Element Research* 136: 127–39.

Baghurst, Peter A., Anthony J. McMichael, Neil R. Wigg, Graham V. Vimpani, Evelyn F. Robertson, Russell J. Roberts, and Shi-Lu Tong. 1992. "Environmental Exposure to Lead and Children's Intelligence at the Age of Seven Years: The Port Pirie Cohort Study." NEJM 327: 1279–84.

Calder, Ian C., David M. Roder, Adrian J. Esterman, Milton J. Lewis, Malcolm C. Harrison, and Robert K. Oldfield. 1986. "Blood Lead Levels in Children in the North-West of Adelaide." *Medical Journal of Australia* 144 (10): 509–12.

Caravanos, Jack, Edith E. Clarke, Carl S. Osei, and Yaw Amoyaw-Osei. 2013. "Exploratory Health Assessment of Chemical Exposures at E-Waste Recycling and Scrapyard Facility in Ghana." *Journal of Health and Pollution* 3 (4): 11–22. https://doi.org/10.5696/2156-9614-3.4.11.

Caravanos, Jack, Russell Dowling, Martha María Téllez-Rojo Dra, Alejandra Cantoral, Roni Kobrosly, Daniel Estrada, Manuela Orjuela, Sandra Gualtero, Bret Ericson, Anthony Rivera, and Richard Fuller. 2014. "Blood Lead Levels in Mexico and Pediatric Burden of Disease Implications." *Annals of Global Health* 80 (4): 269–77.

Counter, S. A., L. H. Buchanan, G. Laurell, and F. Ortega. 1998. "Field Screening of Blood Lead Levels in Remote Andean Villages." *Neurotoxicology* 19 (6): 871–77.

Daniell, William E., Lo Van Tung, Ryan M. Wallace, Deborah J. Havens, Catherine J. Karr, Nguyen Bich Diep, Gerry A. Croteau, Nancy J. Beaudet, and Nguyen Duy Bao. 2015. "Childhood Lead Exposure from Battery Recycling in Vietnam." *BioMed Research International* 2015: 193715. http://dx.doi.org/10.1155/2015/193715.

Gao, Wanzhen, Zhu Lia, Rachel B. Kaufmann, Robert L. Jones, Zhengang Wang, Yafen Chen, Xiuqin Zhao, and Naifen Wang. 2001. "Blood Lead Levels among Children Aged 1 to 5 Years in Wuxi City, China." *Environmental Research* 87 (1): 11–19.

Grigoryan, Ruzanna, Varduhi Petrosyan, Dzovinar Melkom Melkomian, Vahe Khachadourian, Andrew McCartor, and Byron Crape. 2016. "Risk Factors for Children's Blood Lead Levels in Metal Mining and Smelting Communities in Armenia: A Cross-Sectional Study." *BMC Public Health* 16: 945. doi:10.1186/s12889-016-3613-9.

Ibeto, C. N., and C. O. B. Okoye. 2010. "High Levels of Heavy Metals in Blood of the Urban Population in Nigeria." *Research Journal of Environmental Sciences* 4 (4): 371– 82.

Jasso-Pineda, Yolanda, Guillermo Espinosa-Reyes, Donají González-Mille, Israel Razo-Soto, Leticia Carrizales, Arturo Torres-Dosal, Jesús Mejía-Saavedra, Marcos Monroy, Ana Irina Ize, Mario Yarto, and Fernando Díaz-Barriga. 2007. "An Integrated Health Risk Assessment

Approach to the Study of Mining Sites Contaminated with Arsenic and Lead." *Integrated Environmental Assessment and Management* 3 (3): 344–50.

Jones, Donald E., Assane Diop, Meredith Block, Alexander Smith-Jones, and Andrea Smith-Jones 2011. "Assessment and Remediation of Lead Contamination in Senegal." *Blacksmith Institute Journal of Health & Pollution* 1 (2): 37–47.

Lo, Yi-Chun, Carrie A. Dooyema, Antonio Neri, James Durant, Taran Jefferies, Andrew Medina-Marino, Lori de Ravello, Douglas Thoroughman, Lora Davis, Raymond S. Dankoli, Matthias Y. Samson, Luka M. Ibrahim, Ossai Okechukwu, Nasir T. Umar-Tsafe, Alhassan H. Dama, and Mary Jean Brown. 2012. "Childhood Lead Poisoning Associated with Gold Ore Processing: A Village-Level Investigation—Zamfara State, Nigeria, October–November 2010." *Environmental Health Perspectives* 120 (10): 1450–55.

Malcoe, Lorraine Halinka, Robert A. Lynch, Michelle Crozier Keger, and Valerie J. Skaggs. 2002. "Lead Sources, Behaviors, and Socioeconomic Factors in Relation to Blood Lead of Native American and White Children: A Community-Based Assessment of a Former Mining Area." *Environmental Health Perspectives* 110 (Supplement 2): 221–31.

Qu, Chang-Sheng, Zong-Wei Ma, Jin Yang, Yang Liu, Jun Bi, and Lei Huang. 2012. "Human Exposure Pathways of Heavy Metals in a Lead-Zinc Mining Area, Jiangsu Province, China." *PLOS ONE* 7 (11) e46793.

Riddell, Travis J, Orville Solon, Stella A. Quimbo, Cheryl May C. Tan, Elizabeth Butrick, and John W. Peabody. 2007. "Elevated Blood-Lead Levels among Children Living in the Rural Philippines." *Bulletin of the World Health Organization* 85 (9): 674–82.

Röllin, Halina B., Cibele V. C. Rudge, Yngvar Thomassen, Angela Mathee, and Jon Ø. Odland. 2009. "Levels of Toxic and Essential Metals in Maternal and Umbilical Cord Blood from Selected Areas of South Africa—Results of a Pilot Study." *J. Environ. Monit.* 11: 618–27.

Sanders, Alison P., Sloane K. Miller, Viet Nguyen, Jonathan B. Kotch, and Rebecca C. Fry. 2014. "Toxic Metal Levels in Children Residing in a Smelting Craft Village in Vietnam: A Pilot Biomonitoring Study." *BMC Public Health* 14: 114.

Solon, Orville, Travis J. Riddell, Stella A. Quimbo, Elizabeth Butrick, Glen P. Aylward, Marife Lou Bacate, and John W. Peabody. 2008. "Associations between Cognitive Function, Blood Lead Concentration, and Nutrition among Children in the Central Philippines." *Journal of Pediatrics* 152 (2): 237–43.

Suvd, Duvjir Suvd, Rendoo Davaadorj, Dayanjav Baatartsol, Surenjav Unursaikhan, Myagmar Tsengelmaa, Tsogbayar Oyu, Sonom Yunden, Ana M. Hagan-Rogers, and Stephan Böse-O'Reilly. 2015. "Toxicity Assessment in Artisanal Miners from Low-Level Mercury Exposure in Bornuur and Jargalant Soums of Mongolia." *Procedia Environmental Sciences* 30: 97–102.

Thakur, Jarnail Singh, Shankar Prinja, Dalbir Singh, Arvind Rajwanshi, Rajendra Prasad, Harjinder Kaur Parwana, and Rajesh Kumar. 2010. "Adverse Reproductive and Child Health Outcomes among People Living near Highly Toxic Waste Water Drains in Punjab, India." *J. Epidemiol. Community Health* 64: 148e–154. doi:10.1136/jech.2008.078568.

Were, Faridah Hussein, Wilson Njue, Jane Murung, and Ruth Wanjau. 2008. "Use of Human Nails as Bio-Indicators of Heavy Metals Environmental Exposure among School Age Children in Kenya." *Science of the Total Environment* 393 (2–3): 376–84.

Xie, Xiao-hua, Zang-wen Tan, Ni Jia, Zhao-yang Fan, Shuai-ming Zhang, Yan-yu Lü, Li Chen, and Yao-hua Dai. 2013. "Blood Lead Levels among Children Aged 0 to 6 Years in 16 Cities of China, 2004-2008." *Chinese Medical Journal* 126 (12): 2291–95. doi:10.3760/cma.j.issn.0366-6999.20122327.

Resources for Health-Outcomes Assessment

This appendix provides links to resources for evaluating methods for assessing specific health outcomes (see the Bickley reference below and table E.1). Note that intermediate health outcomes evaluated using biomarkers are discussed in chapter 4 and appendix D, which focus on sampling in biological matrixes for biomarkers of exposure, effect, or both exposure and effect.

Bickley, L. S. 2012. Bates' *Guide to Examination and History Taking,* 11th ed. Philadelphia: Lippincott Williams & Wilkins, an imprint of Wolters Kluwer.	Interviewing and obtaining a health history

TABLE E.1 **Links to resources for health-outcomes assessment**

REFERENCE	HEALTH OUTCOME
Pulmonary function testing	
"Pulmonary Function Testing," American Thoracic Society website, https://www.thoracic.org/	Recommended guidelines for pulmonary-function testing (PFT)
Ranu, H., M. Wilde, and B. Madden. 2011. "Pulmonary Function Tests." *Ulster Medical Journal* 80 (2): 84–90. https://www.ncbi.nlm.nih.gov/pmc/articles/PMC3229853/	Overview of PFTs, including references to European and US reference and guidance manuals
Higashimoto, Y., T. Iwata, M. Okada, H. Satoh, K. Fukuda, and Y. Tohda. 2009. "Serum Biomarkers as Predictors of Lung Function Decline in Chronic Obstructive Pulmonary Disease." *Respiratory Medicine* 103 (8): 1231–38. https://www.resmedjournal.com/article/S0954-6111(09)00037-7/fulltext	Discussion of the utility of C-reactive protein (CRP) for predicting lung function
Renal outcomes in children and adults	
National Kidney Foundation website, https://www.kidney.org/	Official guidance from the National Kidney Foundation (US) on standard renal-panel testing and interpretation in urine samples

continued

TABLE E.1, *continued*

REFERENCE	HEALTH OUTCOME
Swedish Council on Health Technology Assessment (SBU). 2013. "Methods to Estimate and Measure Renal Function (Glomerular Filtration Rate): A Systematic Review." Yellow Report No. 214, SBU, Stockholm. https://www.ncbi.nlm.nih.gov/books/NBK285322/pdf/Bookshelf_NBK285322.pdf	Creatinine-based equations from the Modification of Diet in Renal Disease Study (MDRD), the Chronic Kidney Disease Epidemiology Collaboration (CKD-EPI), and the revised Lund-Malmö equation (LM-rev) are all accurate (P30 ≥ 75%) for estimating kidney function in adults, except in patients with GFR < 30 mL/min/1.73 m² or BMI < 20 kg/m². Cockcroft-Gault (CG) should not be used.
Argyropoulos, C. P., S. S. Chen, Y. H. Ng, M. E Roumelioti, K. Shaffi, P. P. Singh, and A. H. Tzamaloukas. 2017. "Rediscovering Beta-2 Microglobulin as a Biomarker Across the Spectrum of Kidney Diseases." *Frontiers in Medicine* 4: 73. https://www.frontiersin.org/articles/10.3389/fmed.2017.00073/full	Background and justification for use of beta-2-microglobulin as a sensitive marker of kidney damage. This is the preferred biomarker of cadmium (Cd) effects recommended by the European Food Safety Authority (EFSA).

Complete blood count

REFERENCE	HEALTH OUTCOME
Keng, T. B., B. De La Salle, G. Bourner, A. Merino, J.-Y. Han, Y. Kawai, M. T. Peng, R. McCafferty, and International Council for Standardization in Haematology (ICSH). 2016. "Standardization of Haematology Critical Results Management in Adults: An International Council for Standardization in Haematology, ICSH, Survey and Recommendations." Int j Lab Hematl 38 (5): 457–71. https://doi.org/10.1111/ijlh.12526	Recommendation for standardization of hematology-reporting units used for complete blood count (CBC)

Neurodevelopmental outcomes in children

REFERENCE	HEALTH OUTCOME
Fernald, L. C. H., E. Prado, P. Kariger, and A. Raikes. 2017. "A Toolkit for Measuring Early Childhood Development in Low- and Middle-Income Countries." World Bank, Washington, DC. https://openknowledge.worldbank.org/handle/10986/29000	Report comes with an Excel spreadsheet to use to help guide selection of appropriate instrument out of 147 possible instruments.
UNESCO (United Nations Educational, Scientific and Cultural Organization). Measuring Early Learning Quality and Outcomes (MELQO). https://www.brookings.edu/wp-content/uploads/2017/06/melqo-measuring-early-learning-quality-outcomes.pdf	Collaborative effort of the MELQO core team, technical advisory groups, and steering committee, describing modules and where they were piloted
Anderson, K., and R. Sayre. 2016. "Measuring Early Learning Quality and Outcomes in Tanzania." Report, Center for Universal Education at Brookings, Washington, DC. https://www.brookings.edu/wp-content/uploads/2017/06/melqo-measuring-early-learning-quality-outcomes-in-tanzania_2016oct.pdf	Application of the MELQO modules and approach in consultation with Ministry of Education in Tanzania, published by the Brookings Institution
Brookings Institution. 2017. "Measuring Early Learning Quality and Outcomes (MELQO)." https://www.brookings.edu/research/measuring-early-learning-quality-and-outcomes-in-tanzania/	Further background and reports on the MELQO effort
World Bank. 2016. "Measuring Early Learning Quality and Outcomes (MELQO) Modules: Quick Guide to Content and Use." https://www.worldbank.org/en/topic/education/brief/ecd-resources	Resource guide for applying the MELQO modules
Abubakar, A., P. Holding, A. Van Baar, C. R. Newton, and F. J. van de Vijver. 2008. "Monitoring Psychomotor Development in a Resource Limited Setting: An Evaluation of the Kilifi Developmental Inventory." *Annals of Tropical Paediatrics* 28 (3): 217–26. https://ora.ox.ac.uk/objects/uuid:b6a43d8c-0d7e-4e01-a2ba-521e4ae33c55	Overview of a psychomotor-testing instrument for use in limited-resource settings
Ballot, D. E., T. Ramdin, D. Rakotsoane, F. Agaba, V. A. Davies, T. Chirwa, and P. A. Cooper. 2017. "Use of the Bayley Scales of Infant and Toddler Development, Third Edition, to Assess Developmental Outcome in Infants and Young Children in an Urban Setting in South Africa." *International Scholarly Research Notices* 2017 (2): 1631760. https://www.ncbi.nlm.nih.gov/pmc/articles/PMC5556991/	Example of an adaptation of a standardized instrument, the Bayley Scales, to South Africa
Dramé, C., and C. J. Ferguson. 2019. "Measurements of Intelligence in Sub-Saharan Africa: Perspectives Gathered from Research in Mali." *Current Psychology* 38: 110–15. https://link.springer.com/article/10.1007/s12144-017-9591-y	Discussion of neurodevelopmental testing approaches used in Mali
Ertem, I. O., D. G. Dogan, C. G. Gok, S. U. Kizilates, A. Caliskan, G. Atay, N. Vatandas, T. Karaaslan, S. G. Baskan, and D. V. Cicchetti. 2008. "A Guide for Monitoring Child Development in Low- and Middle-Income Countries." *Pediatrics* 121 (3): e581–89. https://pediatrics.aappublications.org/content/121/3/e581.short	Overview of testing instruments that have been adapted to low-resource settings

continued

TABLE E.1, *continued*

REFERENCE	HEALTH OUTCOME
Gladstone, M. J., G. A. Lancaster, A. P. Jones, K. Maleta, E. Mtitimila, P. Ashorn, and R. L. Smyth. 2008. "Can Western Developmental Screening Tools be Modified for Use in a Rural Malawian Setting?" *Archives of Disease in Childhood* 93 (1): 23–29. https://adc.bmj.com/content/archdischild/93/1/23.full.pdf?with-ds=yes	Discussion of potential instruments
Gladstone, M., G. A. Lancaster, E. Umar, M. Nyirenda, E. Kayira, N. R. van den Broek, and R. L. Smyth. 2010. "The Malawi Developmental Assessment Tool (MDAT): The Creation, Validation, and Reliability of a Tool to Assess Child Development in Rural African Settings." *PLoS Medicine* 7 (5): e1000273. https://journals.plos.org/plosmedicine/article?id=10.1371/journal.pmed.1000273	Development and application of a testing instrument in Malawi; could be adapted to other locations
Holding, P. A., H. G. Taylor, S. D. Kazungu, T. Mkala, J. Gona, B. Mwamuye, L. Mbonani, and J. Stevenson. 2004. "Assessing Cognitive Outcomes in a Rural African Population: Development of a Neuropsychological Battery in Kilifi District, Kenya." *Journal of the International Neuropsychological Society* 10 (2): 246–60. https://www.cambridge.org/core/journals/journal-of-the-international-neuropsychological-society/article/abs/assessing-cognitive-outcomes-in-a-rural-african-population-development-of-a-neuropsychological-battery-in-kilifi-district-kenya/7B19180497EA3C84AD41C9C1DF476F77	Experience in Kenya developing an instrument for assessing cognitive development
Janus, M., and D. R. Offord. 2007. "Development and Psychometric Properties of the Early Development Instrument (EDI): A Measure of Children's School Readiness." *Canadian Journal of Behavioural Science* 39 (1): 1–22. https://psycnet.apa.org/buy/2007-04967-001	Although developed in a Western context, the Early Development Instrument (EDI) may be adaptable to low-resource settings
McCoy, D. C., M. M. Black, B. Daelmans, and T. Dua. 2016. "Measuring Development in Children from Birth to Age 3 at Population Level." *Early Childhood Matters* 125: 34–39. https://bernardvanleer.org/app/uploads/2016/07/Early-Childhood-Matters-2016_6.pdf	Further background on the ECDI instrument
McCoy, D. C, E. D. Peet, M. Ezzati, G. Danaei, M. M. Black, C. R. Sudfeld, W. Fawzi, and G. Fink. 2016. "Early Childhood Developmental Status in Low- and Middle-Income Countries: National, Regional, and Global Prevalence Estimates Using Predictive Modeling." *PLoS Medicine* 4 (1): e1002233. https://journals.plos.org/plosmedicine/article?id=10.1371/journal.pmed.1002034	Early Childhood Development Instrument (ECDI) suitable for young children; well validated in low-resource settings
McCoy, D. C., C. R. Sudfeld, D. C. Bellinger, A. Muhihi, G. Ashery, T. E. Weary, W. Fawzi, and G. Fink. 2017. "Development and Validation of an Early Childhood Development Scale for Use in Low-Resourced Settings." *Population Health Metrics* 15 (1): 3. https://pophealthmetrics.biomedcentral.com/articles/10.1186/s12963-017-0122-8	Detailed evaluation of ECDI
Oppong, S. 2017. "Contextualizing Psychological Testing in Ghana." *Psychology and Its Context* 8 (1): 3–17. https://www.researchgate.net/publication/327536906_Contextualizing_psychological_testing_in_Ghana	Discussion of the types of tests used in Ghana and the challenge associated with the current state of psychological testing in Ghana
Sabanathan, S., B. Wills, and M. Gladstone. 2015. "Child Development Assessment Tools in Low-Income and Middle-Income Countries: How Can We Use Them More Appropriately?" *Archives of Disease in Childhood* 100 (5): 482–88. https://www.ncbi.nlm.nih.gov/pmc/articles/PMC4413834/pdf/archdischild-2014-308114.pdf	Issues and criteria for application of neurodevelopmental assessment instruments in low-resource settings
Semrud-Clikeman, M., R. A. Romero, E. L. Prado, E. G. Shapiro, P. Bangirana, and C. C. John. 2017. "Selecting Measures for the Neurodevelopmental Assessment of Children in Low- and Middle-Income Countries." *Child Neuropsychology* 23 (7): 761–802. https://www.ncbi.nlm.nih.gov/pmc/articles/PMC5690490/	Issues and criteria for application of neurodevelopmental assessment instruments in low-resource settings
Cardiovascular disease	
Cosselman, K. E., A. Navas-Acien, and J. D. Kaufman. 2015. "Environmental Factors in Cardiovascular Disease." *Nature Reviews Cardiology* 12 (11): 627–42. https://www.nature.com/articles/nrcardio.2015.152	Discussion of lead (Pb), cadmium (Cd), arsenic (As), and cardiovascular disease
Mordukhovich, I., R. O. Wright, H. Hu, C. Amarasiriwardena, A. Baccarelli, A. Litonjua, D. Sparrow, P. Vokonas, and J. Schwartz. 2012. "Associations of Toenail Arsenic, Cadmium, Mercury, Manganese, and Lead with Blood Pressure in the Normative Aging Study." *Environmental Health Perspectives* 120 (1): 98–104. https://www.ncbi.nlm.nih.gov/pmc/articles/PMC3261928/	Observed associations between blood pressure and arsenic (As) and manganese but not the other metals

Source: World Bank compilation.

APPENDIX F

Bibliography

The "Health Outcomes" section of this bibliography lists studies of exposures to metals in relation to health outcomes as well as studies that discuss measurement of outcomes. Subsequent sections focus on studies relevant to used lead-acid batteries (ULAB) and peer-reviewed literature on measurement methods and analysis of metals, particularly in terms of bioaccessibility and bioavailability.

HEALTH OUTCOMES

Metals exposure

Arsenic

Abdul, K. S., S. S. Jayasinghe, E. P. Chandana, C. Jayasumana, and P. M. De Silva. 2015. "Arsenic and Human Health Effects: A Review." *Environmental Toxicology and Pharmacology* 40 (3): 828–46.

Adonis, M., V. Martinez, P. Marin, and L. Gil. 2005. "CYP1A1 and GSTM1 Genetic Polymorphisms in Lung Cancer Populations Exposed to Arsenic in Drinking Water." *Xenobiotica* 35 (5): 519–30.

Ahir, B. K., A. P. Sanders, J. E. Rager, and R. C. Fry. 2013. "Systems Biology and Birth Defects Prevention: Blockade of the Glucocorticoid Receptor Prevents Arsenic-Induced Birth Defects." *Environmental Health Perspectives* 121 (3): 332–38.

Alamolhodaei, N. S., K. Shirani, and G. Karimi. 2015. "Arsenic Cardiotoxicity: An Overview." *Environmental Toxicology and Pharmacology* 40 (3): 1005–14.

Andrade, V. M., M. L. Mateus, M. C. Batoréu, M. Aschner, and A. M. Dos Santos. 2015. "Lead, Arsenic, and Manganese Metal Mixture Exposures: Focus on Biomarkers of Effect." *Biological Trace Element Research* 166 (1): 13–23.

Arita, A., and M. Costa. 2009. "Epigenetics in Metal Carcinogenesis: Nickel, Arsenic, Chromium and Cadmium." *Metallomics* 1 (3): 222–28.

Arslan, B., M. B. Djamgoz, and E. Akün. 2016. "ARSENIC: A Review on Exposure Pathways, Accumulation, Mobility and Transmission into the Human Food Chain." In *Reviews of Environmental Contamination and Toxicology* 243: 27–51.

Bailey, K., and R. C. Fry. 2014. "Long-Term Health Consequences of Prenatal Arsenic Exposure: Links to the Genome and the Epigenome." *Reviews on Environmental Health* 29 (1–2): 9–12.

Bailey, K. A., A. H. Smith, E. J. Tokar, J. H. Graziano, K.-W. Kim, P. Navasumrit, M. Ruchirawat, A. Thiantanawat, W. A. Suk, and R. C. Fry. 2016. "Mechanisms Underlying Latent Disease Risk Associated with Early-Life Arsenic Exposure: Current Research Trends and Scientific Gaps." *Environmental Health Perspectives* 124 (2): 170–75.

Brender, J. D., L. Suarez, M. Felkner, Z. Gilani, D. Stinchcomb, K. Moody, J. Henry, and K. Hendricks. 2006. "Maternal Exposure to Arsenic, Cadmium, Lead, and Mercury and Neural Tube Defects in Offspring." *Environmental Research* 101 (1): 132–29.

Cubadda, F., B. P. Jackson, K. L. Cottingham, Y. O. Van Horne, and M. Kurzius-Spencer. 2017. "Human Exposure to Dietary Inorganic Arsenic and Other Arsenic Species: State of Knowledge, Gaps and Uncertainties." *Science of the Total Environment* 579: 1228–39.

de Burbure, C. D., J.-P. Buchet, A. Bernard, A. Leroyer, C. Nisse, J.-M. Haguenoer, E. Bergamaschi, and A. Mutti. 2003. "Biomarkers of Renal Effects in Children and Adults with Low Environmental Exposure to Heavy Metals." *Journal of Toxicology and Environmental Health Part A* 66 (9): 783–98.

de Burbure, C., J.-P. Buchet, A. Leroyer, C. Nisse, J.-M. Haguenoer, A. Mutti, Z. Smerhovský, Miroslav Cikrt, Malgorzata Trzcinka-Ochocka, Grazyna Razniewska, Marek Jakubowski, and Alfred Bernard. 2006. "Renal and Neurologic Effects of Cadmium, Lead, Mercury, and Arsenic in Children: Evidence of Early Effects and Multiple Interactions at Environmental Exposure Levels." *Environmental Health Perspectives* 114 (4): 584–90.

de la Calle, M. B., V. Devesa, Y. Fiamegos, and D. Vélez. 2017. "Determination of Inorganic Arsenic in a Wide Range of Food Matrices using Hydride Generation: Atomic Absorption Spectrometry." *Journal of Visualized Experiments* 2017 (127): e55953. doi:10.3791/55953.

DeSesso, J., C. Jacobson, A. Scialli, C. Farr, and J. Holson. 1998. "An Assessment of the Developmental Toxicity of Inorganic Arsenic." *Reproductive Toxicology* 12 (4): 385–433.

Fiamegkos, I., F. Cordeiro, P. Robouch, D. Vélez, V. Devesa, G. Raber, J. J. Sloth, R. R. Rasmussen, T. Llorente-Mirandes, J. F. Lopez-Sanchez, R. Rubio, F. Cubadda, M. D'Amato, J. Feldmann, A. Raab, H. Emteborg, and M. B. de la Callea. 2016. "Accuracy of a Method Based on Atomic Absorption Spectrometry to Determine Inorganic Arsenic in Food: Outcome of the Collaborative Trial IMEP-41." *Food Chemistry* 213: 169–79.

Flora, S. J., and S. Agrawal. 2017. "Arsenic, Cadmium, and Lead." In *Reproductive and Developmental Toxicology* 2nd ed., edited by R. C. Gupta, 537–66. London: Academic Press, an imprint of Elsevier.

Gamboa-Loira, B., M. E. Cebrián, F. Franco-Marina, and L. López-Carrillo. 2017. "Arsenic Metabolism and Cancer Risk: A Meta-Analysis." *Environmental Research* 156: 551–58.

Golub, M. S., M. S. Macintosh, and N. Baumrind. 1998. "Developmental and Reproductive Toxicity of Inorganic Arsenic: Animal Studies and Human Concerns." *Journal of Toxicology and Environmental Health, Part B Critical Reviews* 1 (3): 199–237.

Grau-Pérez, M., C.-C. Kuo, M. Spratlen, K. A. Thayer, M. A. Mendez, R. F. Hamman, D. Dabelea, John L. Adgate, William C. Knowler, Ronny A. Bell, Frederick W. Miller, Angela D. Liese, Chongben Zhang, Christelle Douillet, Zuzana Drobná, Elizabeth J. Mayer-Davis, Miroslav Styblo, and Ana Navas-Acien. 2017. "The Association of Arsenic Exposure and Metabolism with Type 1 and Type 2 Diabetes in Youth: The SEARCH Case-Control Study." *Diabetes Care* 40 (1): 46–53.

Hata, A., H. Kurosawa, Y. Endo, K. Yamanaka, N. Fujitani, and G. Endo. 2010. "A Biological Indicator of Inorganic Arsenic Exposure Using the Sum of Urinary Inorganic Arsenic and Monomethylarsonic Acid Concentrations." *Journal of Occupational Health* 58 (2): 196–200.

Hays, S. M., L. L. Aylward, M. Gagné, A. Nong, and K. Krishnan. 2010. "Biomonitoring Equivalents for Inorganic Arsenic." *Regulatory Toxicology and Pharmacology* 58 (1): 1–9.

Jansen, R. J., M. Argos, L. Tong, J. Li, M. Rakibuz-Zaman, M. T. Islam, V. Slavkovich, Alauddin Ahmed, Ana Navas-Acien, Faruque Parvez, Yu Chen, Mary V. Gamble, Joseph H. Graziano, Brandon L. Pierce, and Habibul Ahsan. 2015. "Determinants and Consequences of Arsenic Metabolism Efficiency among 4,794 Individuals: Demographics, Lifestyle, Genetics, and Toxicity." *Cancer Epidemiology and Prevention Biomarkers* 25 (2): 381–90.

Jones, M. R., M. Tellez-Plaza, D. Vaidya, M. Grau, K. A. Francesconi, W. Goessler, E. Guallar, W. S. Post, J. D. Kaufman, and A. Navas-Acien. 2016. "Estimation of Inorganic Arsenic Exposure in Populations with Frequent Seafood Intake: Evidence From MESA and NHANES." *American Journal of Epidemiology* 184 (8): 590–602.

Kadono, T., T. Inaoka, N. Murayama, K. Ushijima, M. Nagano, S. Nakamura, C. Watanabe, K. Tamaki, and R. Ohtsuka. 2002. "Skin Manifestations of Arsenicosis in Two Villages in Bangladesh." *International Journal of Dermatology* 41 (12): 841–46.

Karagas, M. R., C. X. Le, S. T. Morris, J. O. Blum, X. I. Lu, V. I. Spate, M. A. Carey, V. I. Stannard, B. J. Klaue, and T. D. Tosteson. 2001. "Markers of Low Level Arsenic Exposure for Evaluating Human Cancer Risks in a US Population." *International Journal of Occupational Medicine and Environmental Health* 14 (2): 171–75.

Karagas, M. R., T. D. Tosteson, J. S. Morris, E. Demidenko, L. A. Mott, J. Heaney, and A. Schned. 2004. "Incidence of Transitional Cell Carcinoma of the Bladder and Arsenic Exposure in New Hampshire." *Cancer Causes & Control* 15 (5): 465–72.

Kuo, C-C., K. A. Moon, S. L. Wang, E. Silbergeld, and A. Navas-Acien. 2017. "The Association of Arsenic Metabolism with Cancer, Cardiovascular Disease, and Diabetes: A Systematic Review of the Epidemiological Evidence." *Environmental Health Perspectives* 125 (8): 087001.

Liu, L., J. R. Trimarchi, P. Navarro, M. A. Blasco, and D. L. Keefe. 2003. "Oxidative Stress Contributes to Arsenic-Induced Telomere Attrition, Chromosome Instability, and Apoptosis." *Journal of Biological Chemistry* 278 (34): 31998–2004.

Lynch, H. N., G. I. Greenberg, M. C. Pollock, and A. S. Lewis. 2014. "A Comprehensive Evaluation of Inorganic Arsenic in Food and Considerations for Dietary Intake Analyses." *Science of the Total Environment* 496: 299–313.

Marchiset-Ferlay, N., C. Savanovitch, and M. P. Sauvant-Rochat. 2012. "What Is the Best Biomarker to Assess Arsenic Exposure via Drinking Water?" *Environment International* 39 (1): 150–71.

Martinez, V. D., E. A. Vucic, D. D. Becker-Santos, L. Gil, and W. L. Lam. 2011. "Arsenic Exposure and the Induction of Human Cancers." *Journal of Toxicology* 2011 (5576): 431287.

Martínez-Sánchez, M. J., S. Martínez-López, L. B. Martínez-Martínez, and C. Pérez-Sirvent. 2013. "Importance of the Oral Arsenic Bioaccessibility Factor for Characterising the Risk Associated with Soil Ingestion in a Mining-Influenced Zone." *Journal of Environmental Management* 116: 10–17.

Michaud, D. S., M. E. Wright, K. P. Cantor, P. R. Taylor, J. Virtamo, and D. Albanes. 2004. "Arsenic Concentrations in Prediagnostic Toenails and the Risk of Bladder Cancer in a Cohort Study of Male Smokers." *American Journal of Epidemiology* 160 (9): 853–39.

Minatel, B. C., A. P. Sage, C. Anderson, R. Hubaux, E. A. Marshall, W. L. Lam, and V. D. Martinez. 2018. "Environmental Arsenic Exposure: From Genetic Susceptibility to Pathogenesis." *Environment International* 112: 183–97.

Naujokas, M. F., B. Anderson, H. Ahsan, H. V. Aposhian, J. H. Graziano, C. Thompson, and W. A. Suk. 2013. "The Broad Scope of Health Effects from Chronic Arsenic Exposure: Update on a Worldwide Public Health Problem." *Environmental Health Perspectives* 121 (3): 295–302.

Navas-Acien, A., E. K. Silbergeld, R. A. Streeter, J. M. Clark, T. A. Burke, and E. Guallar. 2006. "Arsenic Exposure and Type 2 Diabetes: A Systematic Review of the Experimental and Epidemiologic Evidence." *Environmental Health Perspectives* 114 (5): 641–48.

Nordberg, G. F., T. Jin, F. Hong, A. Zhang, F. P. Buchet, and B. Bernard. 2005. "Biomarkers of Cadmium and Arsenic Interactions." *Toxicology and Applied Pharmacology* 206 (2): 191–97.

Putila, J. J., and N. L. Guo. 2011. "Association of Arsenic Exposure with Lung Cancer Incidence Rates in the United States." *PLoS One* 6 (10): e25886.

Rasheed, H., R. Slack, and P. Kay. 2016. "Human Health Risk Assessment for Arsenic: A Critical Review." *Critical Reviews in Environmental Science and Technology* 46 (19–20): 1529–83.

Ray, P. D., A. Yosim, and R. C. Fry. 2014. "Incorporating Epigenetic Data into the Risk Assessment Process for the Toxic Metals Arsenic, Cadmium, Chromium, Lead, and Mercury: Strategies and Challenges." *Frontiers in Genetics* 5: Article 201.

Ren, X., C. M. McHale, C. F. Skibola, A. H. Smith, M. T. Smith, and L. Zhang. 2011. "An Emerging Role for Epigenetic Dysregulation in Arsenic Toxicity and Carcinogenesis." *Environmental Health Perspectives* 119 (1): 11–19.

Sanchez, T. R., M. Perzanowski, and J. H. Graziano. 2016. "Inorganic Arsenic and Respiratory Health, from Early Life Exposure to Sex-Specific Effects: A Systematic Review." *Environmental Research* 147: 537–55.

Shalat, S. L., D. B. Walker, and R. H. Finnell. 1996. "Role of Arsenic as a Reproductive Toxin with Particular Attention to Neural Tube Defects." *Journal of Toxicology and Environmental Health* 48 (3): 253–72.

Shen, H., Q. Niu, M. Xu, D. Rui, S. Xu, G. Feng, Y. Ding, S. Li, and M. Jing. 2016. "Factors Affecting Arsenic Methylation in Arsenic-Exposed Humans: A Systematic Review and Meta-Analysis." *International Journal of Environmental Research and Public Health* 13 (2): Article 205.

Smith, A. H., and C. M. Steinmaus. 2009. "Health Effects of Arsenic and Chromium in Drinking Water: Recent Human Findings." *Annual Review of Public Health* 2009 (30): 107–22.

Spratlen, M. J., M. V. Gamble, M. Grau-Perez, C.-C. Kuo, L. G. Best, J. Yracheta, K. Francesconi, Walter Goessler, Yasmin Mossavar-Rahmani, Meghan Hall, Jason G. Umans, Amanda Fretts, and Ana Navas-Acien. 2017. "Arsenic Metabolism and One-Carbon Metabolism at Low-Moderate Arsenic Exposure: Evidence from the Strong Heart Study." *Food and Chemical Toxicology* 105: 387–97.

Tolins, M., M. Ruchirawat, and P. Landrigan. 2014. "The Developmental Neurotoxicity of Arsenic: Cognitive and Behavioral Consequences of Early Life Exposure." *Annals of Global Health* 80 (4): 303–14.

Vahter, M. E. 2007. "Interactions between Arsenic-Induced Toxicity and Nutrition in Early Life." *Journal of Nutrition* 137 (12): 2798–804.

Vahter, M. 2008. "Health Effects of Early Life Exposure to Arsenic." *Basic & Clinical Pharmacology & Toxicology* 102 (2): 204–11.

Vahter, M. 2009. "Effects of Arsenic on Maternal and Fetal Health." *Annual Review of Nutrition* 29 (1): 381–99.

von Ehrenstein, O. S., S. Poddar, Y. Yuan, D. G. Mazumder, B. Eskenazi, A. Basu, M. Hira-Smith, Nalima Ghosh, Sabari Lahiri, Reina Haque, Alakendu Ghosh, Dave Kalman, Subankar Das, and Allan H. Smith. 2007. "Children's Intellectual Function in Relation to Arsenic Exposure." *Epidemiology* 18 (1): 44–51.

Wang, G., and B. A. Fowler. 2008. "Roles of Biomarkers in Evaluating Interactions among Mixtures of Lead, Cadmium and Arsenic." *Toxicology and Applied Pharmacology* 233 (1): 92–99.

Weidemann, D., C.-C. Kuo, A. Navas-Acien, A. G. Abraham, V. Weaver, and J. Fadrowski. 2015. "Association of Arsenic with Kidney Function in Adolescents and Young Adults: Results from the National Health and Nutrition Examination Survey 2009–2012." *Environmental Research* 140: 317–24.

Yager, J. W., T. Greene, and R. A. Schoof. 2015. "Arsenic Relative Bioavailability from Diet and Airborne Exposures: Implications for Risk Assessment." *Science of the Total Environment* 536: 368–81.

Lead

Aboh, I. J., M. A. Sampson, L. A. Nyaab, J. Caravanos, F. G. Ofosu, and H. Kuranchie-Mensah. 2013. "Assessing Levels of Lead Contamination in Soil and Predicting Pediatric Blood Lead Levels in Tema, Ghana." *Journal of Health and Pollution* 3 (5): 7–12.

Andrade, V. M., M. L. Mateus, M. C. Batoréu, M. Aschner, and A. M. Dos Santos. 2015. "Lead, Arsenic, and Manganese Metal Mixture Exposures: Focus on Biomarkers of Effect." *Biological Trace Element Research* 166 (1): 13–23.

Barbosa, F. Jr., J. E. Tanus-Santos, R. F. Gerlach, and P. J. Parsons. 2005. "A Critical Review of Biomarkers Used for Monitoring Human Exposure to Lead: Advantages, Limitations, and Future Needs." *Environmental Health Perspectives* 113 (12): 1669–74.

Binstock, D. A., W. F. Gutknecht, and A. C. McWilliams. 2009. "Lead in Soil—An Examination of Paired XRF Analysis Performed in the Field and Laboratory ICP-AES Results." *International Journal of Soil, Sediment and Water* 2 (2): Article 1.

Brender, J. D., L. Suarez, M. Felkner, Z. Gilani, D. Stinchcomb, K. Moody, J. Henry, and K. Hendricks. 2006. "Maternal Exposure to Arsenic, Cadmium, Lead, and Mercury and Neural Tube Defects in Offspring." *Environmental Research* 101 (1): 132–39.

Daniell, W. E., L. Van Tung, R. M. Wallace, D. J. Havens, C. J. Karr, N. Bich Diep, G. A. Croteau, N. J. Beaudet, and N. Duy Bao. 2015. "Childhood Lead Exposure from Battery Recycling in Vietnam." *BioMed Research International* 2015 (9): 193715.

de Burbure, C. D., J.-P. Buchet, A. Bernard, A. Leroyer, C. Nisse, J.-M. Haguenoer, E. Bergamaschi, and A. Mutti. 2003. "Biomarkers of Renal Effects in Children and Adults with Low Environmental Exposure to Heavy Metals." *Journal of Toxicology and Environmental Health Part A* 66 (9): 783–98.

de Burbure, C., J.-P. Buchet, A. Leroyer, C. Nisse, J.-M. Haguenoer, A. Mutti, Z. Smerhovský, Miroslav Cikrt, Malgorzata Trzcinka-Ochocka, Grazyna Razniewska, Marek Jakubowski, and Alfred Bernard. 2006. "Renal and Neurologic Effects of Cadmium, Lead, Mercury, and Arsenic in Children: Evidence of Early Effects and Multiple Interactions at Environmental Exposure Levels." *Environmental Health Perspectives* 114 (4): 584–90.

De Zwart, L. L., B. Klinck, and J. Van Wijnen. 2007. "Comparison of Five *In Vitro* Digestion Models to *In Vivo* Experimental Results: Lead Bioaccessibility in the Human Gastrointestinal Tract." *Journal of Environmental Science and Health Part A* 42 (9): 1203–11.

Ekong, E. B., B. G. Jaar, and V. M. Weaver. 2006. "Lead-Related Nephrotoxicity: A Review of the Epidemiologic Evidence." *Kidney international* 70 (12): 2074–84.

Ericson, B., P. P. Landrigan, M. P. Taylor, J. Frostad, J. Caravanos, J. Keith, and R. Fuller. 2016. "The Global Burden of Lead Toxicity Attributable to Informal Used Lead-Acid Battery Sites." *Annals of Global Health* 82 (5): 686–99.

Flora, S. J., and S. Agrawal. "Arsenic, Cadmium, and Lead." 2017. In *Reproductive and Developmental Toxicology*, 2nd ed., edited by R. C. Gupta, 537–66. London: Academic Press, an imprint of Elsevier.

Hambach, R., D. Lison, P. C. D'Haese, J. Weyler, E. De Graef, A. De Schryver, L. V. Lamberts, and M. Van Sprundel. 2013. "Co-Exposure to Lead Increases the Renal Response to Low Levels of Cadmium in Metallurgy Workers." *Toxicology Letters* 222 (2): 233–38.

Haryanto, B. 2016. "Lead Exposure from Battery Recycling in Indonesia." *Reviews on Environmental Health* 31 (1): 13–16.

Kummrow, F., F. F. Silva, R. Kuno, A. L. Souza, and P. V. Oliveira. 2008. "Biomonitoring Method for the Simultaneous Determination of Cadmium and Lead in Whole Blood by Electrothermal Atomic Absorption Spectrometry for Assessment of Environmental Exposure." *Talanta* 75 (1): 246–52.

Marschner, B., P. Welge, A. Hack, J. Wittsiepe, and M. Wilhelm. 2006. "Comparison of Soil Pb *In Vitro* Bioaccessibility and *In Vivo* Bioavailability with Pb Pools from a Sequential Soil Extraction." *Environmental Science & Technology* 40 (8): 2812–18.

Navas-Acien, A., E. Guallar, E. K. Silbergeld, and S. J. Rothenberg. 2007. "Lead Exposure and Cardiovascular Disease—A Systematic Review." *Environmental Health Perspectives* 115 (3): 472–82.

Nawrot, T. S., L. Thijs, E. M. Den Hond, H. A. Roels, and J. A. Staessen. 2002. "An Epidemiological Re-Appraisal of the Association between Blood Pressure and Blood Lead: A Meta-Analysis." *Journal of Human Hypertension* 16 (2): 123–31.

Ondayo, M. A., G. M. Simiyu, P. O. Raburu, and F. H. Were. 2016. "Child Exposure to Lead in the Vicinities of Informal Used Lead-Acid Battery Recycling Operations in Nairobi Slums, Kenya." *Journal of Health and Pollution* 6 (12): 15–25.

Ray, P. D., A. Yosim, and R. C. Fry. 2014. "Incorporating Epigenetic Data into the Risk Assessment Process for the Toxic Metals Arsenic, Cadmium, Chromium, Lead, and Mercury: Strategies and Challenges." *Frontiers in Genetics* 5: Article 201.

Sanders, T., Y. Liu, V. Buchner, and P. B. Tchounwou. 2009. "Neurotoxic Effects and Biomarkers of Lead Exposure: A Review." *Reviews on Environmental Health* 24 (1): 15–46.

Tsaih, S.-W., S. Korrick, J. Schwartz, C. Amarasiriwardena, A. Aro, D. Sparrow, and H. Hu. 2004. "Lead, Diabetes, Hypertension, and Renal Function: The Normative Aging Study." *Environmental Health Perspectives* 112 (11): 1178–82.

Wang, G., and B. A. Fowler. 2008. "Roles of Biomarkers in Evaluating Interactions among Mixtures of Lead, Cadmium and Arsenic." *Toxicology and Applied Pharmacology* 233 (1): 92–99.

Zahran, S., M. A. Laidlaw, S. P. McElmurry, G. M. Filippelli, and M. Taylor. 2013. "Linking Source and Effect: Resuspended Soil Lead, Air Lead, and Children's Blood Lead Levels in Detroit, Michigan." *Environmental Science & Technology* 47 (6): 2839–45.

Zia, M. H., E. E. Codling, K. G. Scheckel, and R. L. Chaney. 2011. "*In Vitro* and *In Vivo* Approaches for the Measurement of Oral Bioavailability of Lead (Pb) in Contaminated Soils: A Review." *Environmental Pollution* 159 (10): 2320–27.

Measuring neurodevelopmental outcomes

Abubakar, A., P. Holding, A. Van Baar, C. R. Newton, and F. J. van de Vijver. 2008. "Monitoring Psychomotor Development in a Resource Limited Setting: An Evaluation of the Kilifi Developmental Inventory." *Annals of Tropical Paediatrics* 28 (3): 217–26.

Ballot, D. E., T. Ramdin, D. Rakotsoane, F. Agaba, V. A. Davies, T. Chirwa, and P. A. Cooper. 2017. "Use of the Bayley Scales of Infant and Toddler Development, Third Edition, to Assess Developmental Outcome in Infants and Young Children in an Urban Setting in South Africa." *International Scholarly Research Notices* 2017 (2): Article 1631760.

Dramé, C., and C. J. Ferguson. 2019. "Measurements of Intelligence in Sub-Saharan Africa: Perspectives Gathered from Research in Mali." *Current Psychology* 38 (2): 110–16.

Ertem, I. O., D. G. Dogan, C. G. Gok, S. U. Kizilates, A. Caliskan, G. Atay, N. Vatandas, T. Karaaslan, S. G. Baskan, and D. V. Cicchetti. 2008. "A Guide for Monitoring Child Development in Low- and Middle-Income Countries." *Pediatrics* 121 (3): e581–89.

Fernald, L. C., E. Prado, P. Kariger, and A. Raikes. 2017. "A Toolkit for Measuring Early Childhood Development in Low and Middle-Income Countries." Prepared for the Strategic Impact Evaluation Fund, World Bank, Washington, DC. Report comes with an Excel spreadsheet to help guide selection of the appropriate instrument out of 147 possible instruments.

Gladstone, M. J., G. A. Lancaster, A. P. Jones, K. Maleta, E. Mtitimila, P. Ashorn, and R. L. Smyth. 2008. "Can Western Developmental Screening Tools Be Modified for Use in a Rural Malawian Setting?" *Archives of Disease in Childhood* 93 (1): 23–29.

Gladstone, M., G. A. Lancaster, E. Umar, M. Nyirenda, E. Kayira, N. R. van den Broek, and R. L. Smyth. 2010. "The Malawi Developmental Assessment Tool (MDAT): The Creation, Validation, and Reliability of a Tool to Assess Child Development in Rural African Settings." *PLoS Medicine* 7 (5): e1000273.

Holding, P. A., H. G. Taylor, S. D. Kazungu, T. Mkala, J. Gona, B. Mwamuye, L. Mbonani, and J. Stevenson. 2004. "Assessing Cognitive Outcomes in a Rural African Population: Development of a Neuropsychological Battery in Kilifi District, Kenya." *Journal of the International Neuropsychological Society* 10 (2): 246–60.

Janus, M., and D. R. Offord. 2007. "Development and Psychometric Properties of the Early Development Instrument (EDI): A Measure of Children's School Readiness." *Canadian Journal of Behavioural Science* 39 (1): 1–22.

McCoy, D. C., M. M. Black, B. Daelmans, and T. Dua. 2016. "Measuring Development in Children from Birth to Age 3 at Population Level." *Early Childhood Matters* 125: 34–39.

McCoy, D. C., E. D. Peet, M. Ezzati, G. Danaei, M. M. Black, C. R. Sudfeld, W. Fawzi, and G. Fink. 2016. "Early Childhood Developmental Status in Low- and Middle-Income Countries: National, Regional, and Global Prevalence Estimates Using Predictive Modeling." *PLoS Medicine* 13 (6): e1002034.

McCoy, D. C., C. R. Sudfeld, D. C. Bellinger, A. Muhihi, G. Ashery, T. E. Weary, W. Fawzi, and G. Fink. 2017. "Development and Validation of an Early Childhood Development Scale for Use in Low-Resourced Settings." *Population Health Metrics* 15 (1): Article 3.

Oppong, S. 2017. "Contextualizing Psychological Testing in Ghana." *Psychology & Its Contexts* 8 (1): 3–17.

Sabanathan, S., B. Wills, and M. Gladstone. 2015. "Child Development Assessment Tools in Low-Income and Middle-Income Countries: How Can We Use Them More Appropriately?" *Archives of Disease in Childhood* 100 (5): 482–88.

Semrud-Clikeman, M., R. A. Romero, E. L. Prado, E. G. Shapiro, P. Bangirana, and C. C. John. 2017. "Selecting Measures for the Neurodevelopmental Assessment of Children in Low- and Middle-Income Countries." *Child Neuropsychology* 23 (7): 761–802.

Carcinogenic markers

Albertini, R. J., D. Anderson, G. R. Douglas, L. Hagmar, K. Hemminki, F. Merlo, A. T. Natarajan et al. 2000. "IPCS Guidelines for the Monitoring of Genotoxic Effects of Carcinogens in Humans." *Mutation Research/Reviews in Mutation Research* 463 (2): 111–72.

Bonassi, S., L. Hagmar, U. Strömberg, A. H. Montagud, H. Tinnerberg, A. Forni, P. Heikkilä, S. Wanders, P. Wilhardt, I. L. Hansteen, L. E. Knudsen, and H. Norppa. 2000. "Chromosomal Aberrations in Lymphocytes Predict Human Cancer Independently of Exposure to Carcinogens." *Cancer Research* 60 (6): 1619–25.

Bonassi, S., D. Ugolini, M. Kirsch-Volders, U. Strömberg, R. Vermeulen, and J. D. Tucker. 2005. "Human Population Studies with Cytogenetic Biomarkers: Review of the Literature and Future Prospectives." *Environmental and Molecular Mutagenesis* 45 (2–3): 258–70.

Bonassi, S., A. Znaor, M. Ceppi, C. Lando, W. P. Chang, N. Holland, M. Kirsch-Volders, Errol Zeiger, Sadayuki Ban, Roberto Barale, Maria Paola Bigatti, Claudia Bolognesi, Antonina Cebulska-Wasilewska, Eleonora Fabianova, Alexandra Fucic, Lars Hagmar, Gordana Joksic, Antonietta Martelli, Lucia Migliore, Ekaterina Mirkova, Maria Rosaria Scarfi, Andrea Zijno, Hannu Norppa, and Michael Fenech. 2007. "An Increased Micronucleus Frequency in Peripheral Blood Lymphocytes Predict the Risk of Cancer in Humans." *Carcinogenesis* 28 (3): 625–31.

Farmer, P. B., and R. Singh. 2008. "Use of DNA Adducts to Identify Human Health Risk from Exposure to Hazardous Environmental Pollutants: The Increasing Role of Mass Spectrometry in Assessing Biologically Effective Doses of Genotoxic Carcinogens." *Mutation Research/Reviews in Mutation Research* 659 (1): 68–76.

Fenech, M. 2007. "Cytokinesis-Block Micronucleus Cytome Assay." *Nature Protocols* 2 (5): 1084–104. Change per http://cmosshoptalk.com/2018/04/10/316-7-316-17-or-316-317-chicago-style-for-number-ranges/.

Fenech, M., and A. A. Morley. 1985. "Measurement of Micronuclei in Lymphocytes." *Mutation Research/Environmental Mutagenesis and Related Subjects* 147 (1–2): 29–36.

Hagmar, L., S. Bonassi, U. Strömberg, A. Brøgger, L. E. Knudsen, H. Norppa, and C. Reuterwall. 1998. "Chromosomal Aberrations in Lymphocytes Predict Human Cancer: A Report from the European Study Group on Cytogenetic Biomarkers and Health (ESCH)." *Cancer Research* 58 (18): 4117–21.

Cardiovascular

Ahn, J. S., S. Choi, S. H. Jang, H. J. Chang, J. H. Kim, K. B. Nahm, S. W. Oh, and E. Y. Choi. 2003. "Development of a Point-of-Care Assay System for High-Sensitivity C-Reactive Protein in Whole Blood." *Clinica Chimica Acta* 332 (1–2): 51–59.

Cosselman, K. E., A. Navas-Acien, and J. D. Kaufman. 2015. "Environmental Factors in Cardiovascular Disease." *Nature Reviews Cardiology* 12 (11): 627–42.

McDade, T. W., J. Burhop, and J. Dohnal. 2004. "High-Sensitivity Enzyme Immunoassay for C-Reactive Protein in Dried Blood Spots." *Clinical Chemistry* 50 (3): 652–54.

Mordukhovich, I., R. O Wright, H. Hu, C. Amarasiriwardena, A. Baccarelli, A. Litonjua, D. Sparrow, P. Vokonas, and J. Schwartz. 2012. "Associations of Toenail Arsenic, Cadmium, Mercury, Manganese, and Lead with Blood Pressure in the Normative Aging Study." *Environmental Health Perspectives* 120 (1): 98–104.

Ochoa-Martínez, Á. C., E. D. Cardona-Lozano, L. Carrizales-Yáñez, and I. N. Pérez-Maldonado. 2018. "Serum Concentrations of New Predictive Cardiovascular Disease Biomarkers in Mexican Women Exposed to Lead." *Archives of Environmental Contamination and Toxicology* 74 (2): 248–58.

Peña, M. S. B., and A. Rollins. 2017. "Environmental Exposures and Cardiovascular Disease: A Challenge for Health and Development in Low- and Middle-Income Countries." *Cardiology Clinics* 35 (1): 71–86.

Roberts, W. L., L. Moulton, T. C. Law, G. Farrow, M. Cooper-Anderson, J. Savory, and N. Rifai. 2001. "Evaluation of Nine Automated High-Sensitivity C-Reactive Protein Methods: Implications for Clinical and Epidemiological Applications. Part 2." *Clinical Chemistry* 47 (3): 418–25.

Epigenetics

Arita, A., and M. Costa. 2009. "Epigenetics in Metal Carcinogenesis: Nickel, Arsenic, Chromium and Cadmium." *Metallomics* 1 (3): 222–28.

Cheng, T. F., S. Choudhuri, and K. Muldoon-Jacobs. 2012. "Epigenetic Targets of Some Toxicologically Relevant Metals: A Review of the Literature." *Journal of Applied Toxicology* 32 (9): 643–53.

Ercal, N., H. Gurer-Orhan, and N. Aykin-Burns. 2001. "Toxic Metals and Oxidative Stress Part I: Mechanisms Involved in Metal-Induced Oxidative Damage." *Current Topics in Medicinal Chemistry* 1 (6): 529–39.

Fragou, D., A. Fragou, S. Kouidou, S. Njau, and L. Kovatsi. 2011. "Epigenetic Mechanisms in Metal Toxicity." *Toxicology Mechanisms and Methods* 21 (4): 343–52.

Martinez-Zamudio, R., and H. C. Ha. 2011. "Environmental Epigenetics in Metal Exposure." *Epigenetics* 6 (7): 820–27.

Ryu, H.-W., D. H. Lee, H.-R. Won, K. H. Kim, Y. J. Seong, and S. H. Kwon. 2015. "Influence of Toxicologically Relevant Metals on Human Epigenetic Regulation." *Toxicological Research* 31 (1): 1–9.

Fetal growth

Sabra, S., E. Malmqvist, A. Saborit, E. Gratacós, and M. D. Roig. 2017. "Heavy Metals Exposure Levels and their Correlation with Different Clinical Forms of Fetal Growth Restriction." *PLoS One* 12 (10): e0185645.

Anemia

Balarajan, Y., U. Ramakrishnan, E. Özaltin, A. H. Shankar, and S. V. Subramanian. 2012. "Anaemia in Low-Income and Middle-Income Countries." *The Lancet* 378 (9809): 2123–35.

Parker, M., Z. Han, E. Abu-Haydar, E. Matsiko, D. Iyakaremye, L. Tuyisenge, A. Magaret, and A. Lyambabaje. 2018. "An Evaluation of Hemoglobin Measurement Tools and Their Accuracy and Reliability When Screening for Child Anemia in Rwanda: A Randomized Study." *PLoS One* 13 (1): e0187663

Sanchis-Gomar, F., J. Cortell-Ballester, H. Pareja-Galeano, G. Banfi, and G. Lippi. 2013. "Hemoglobin Point-of-Care Testing: the HemoCue System." *Journal of Laboratory Automation* 18 (3): 198–205.

Sharman, A. 2000. "Anemia Testing in Population-Based Surveys: General Information and Guidelines for Country Monitors and Program Managers." Guidance publication for the MEASURE DHS+ project, ORC Macro, Calverton, MD.

Yang, X., N. Z. Piety, S. M. Vignes, M. S. Benton, J. Kanter, and S. S. Shevkoplyas. 2013. "Simple Paper-Based Test for Measuring Blood Hemoglobin Concentration in Resource-Limited Settings." *Clinical Chemistry* 59 (10): 1506–13.

Renal outcomes

D'Amico, G., and C. Bazzi. 2003. "Urinary Protein and Enzyme Excretion as Markers of Tubular Damage." *Current Opinion in Nephrology and Hypertension* 12 (6): 639–43.

Earley, A., D. Miskulin, E. J. Lamb, A. S. Levey, and K. Uhlig. 2012. "Estimating Equations for Glomerular Filtration Rate in the Era of Creatinine Standardization." *Annals of Internal Medicine* 156 (11): 785–95.

Lamb, E. J., F. MacKenzie, and P. E. Stevens. 2009. "How Should Proteinuria Be Detected and Measured?" *Annals of Clinical Biochemistry* 46 (3): 205–17.

Levey, A. S., L. A. Stevens, C. H. Schmid, Y. L. Zhang, A. F. Castro, H. I. Feldman, J. W. Kusek, Paul Eggers, Frederick Van Lente, Tom Greene, and Josef Coresh. 2009. "A New Equation to Estimate Glomerular Filtration Rate." *Annals of Internal Medicine* 150 (9): 604–12.

Prigent, A. 2008. "Monitoring Renal Function and Limitations of Renal Function Tests." *Seminars in Nuclear Medicine* 38 (1): 32–46.

SBU (Swedish Council on Health Technology Assessment). 2013. "Methods to Estimate and Measure Renal Function (Glomerular Filtration Rate) A Systematic Review." Yellow Report No. 214, SBU, Stockholm. https://www.ncbi.nlm.nih.gov/pubmedhealth/PMH0078717 /pdf/PubMedHealth_PMH0078717.pdf.

Traynor, J., R. Mactier, C. C. Geddes, and J. G. Fox. 2006. "How to Measure Renal Function in Clinical Practice." *BMJ* 333 (7571): 733–37.

Weaver, V. M., D. J. Kotchmar, J. J. Fadrowski, and E. K. Silbergeld. 2016. "Challenges for Environmental Epidemiology Research: Are Biomarker Concentrations Altered by Kidney Function or Urine Concentration Adjustment?" *Journal of Exposure Science and Environmental Epidemiology* 26 (1): 1–8.

Lung and lung function

Higashimoto, Y., T. Iwata, M. Okada, H. Satoh, K. Fukuda, and Y. Tohda. 2009. "Serum Biomarkers as Predictors of Lung Function Decline in Chronic Obstructive Pulmonary Disease." *Respiratory Medicine* 103 (8): 1231–38.

General

Barnett-Itzhaki, Z., M. E. López, N. Puttaswamy, and T. Berman. 2018. "A Review of Human Biomonitoring in Selected Southeast Asian Countries." *Environment international* 116: 156–64.

Bernard, A. 2008. "Biomarkers of Metal Toxicity in Population Studies: Research Potential and Interpretation Issues." *Journal of Toxicology and Environmental Health, Part A* 71 (18): 1259–65.

Boerma, J. T., E. Holt, and R. Black. 2001. "Measurement of Biomarkers in Surveys in Developing Countries: Opportunities and Problems." *Population and Development Review* 27 (2): 303–14.

Brindle, E., M. Fujita, J. Shofer, and K. A. O'Connor. 2010. "Serum, Plasma, and Dried Blood Spot High-Sensitivity C-Reactive Protein Enzyme Immunoassay for Population Research." *Journal of Immunological Methods* 362 (1–2): 112–20.

Crimmins, E. M., J. D. Faul, J. K. Kim, and D. R. Weir. 2017. "Documentation of Blood-Based Biomarkers in the 2014 Health and Retirement Study." Report, Survey Research Center, Institute for Social Research, University of Michigan, Ann Arbor.

Crimmins, E., J. K. Kim, H. McCreath, J. Faul, D. Weir, and T. Seeman. 2014. "Validation of Blood-Based Assays Using Dried Blood Spots for Use in Large Population Studies." *Biodemography and Social Biology* 60 (1): 38–48. doi:10.1080/19485565.2014.901885.

Delahaye, L., B. Janssens, and C. Stove. 2017. "Alternative Sampling Strategies for the Assessment of Biomarkers of Exposure." *Current Opinion in Toxicology* 4: 43–51.

Ercal, N., H. Gurer-Orhan, and N. Aykin-Burns. 2001. "Toxic Metals and Oxidative Stress Part I: Mechanisms Involved in Metal-Induced Oxidative Damage." *Current Topics in Medicinal Chemistry* 1 (6): 529–39.

Esteban, M., and A. Castaño. 2009. "Non-Invasive Matrices in Human Biomonitoring: A Review." *Environment International* 35 (2): 438–49.

FDA and NIH (US Food and Drug Administration and National Institutes of Health). 2016. "BEST (Biomarkers, EndpointS, and other Tools) Resource." Glossary copublished by the FDA, Silver Spring, MD; and NIH, Bethesda, MD. https://www.ncbi.nlm.nih.gov/books /NBK326791/.

Freeman, J. D., L. M. Rosman, J. D. Ratcliff, P. T. Strickland, D. R. Graham, and E. K. Silbergeld. 2017. "State of the Science in Dried Blood Spots." *Clinical Chemistry* 64 (4): 656–79. doi:10.1373/clinchem.2017.275966.

Funk, W. E., J. D. Pleil, D. J. Sauter, T. McDade, and J. L. Holl. 2015. "Use of Dried Blood Spots for Estimating Children's Exposures to Heavy Metals in Epidemiological Research." *Journal of Environmental & Analytical Toxicology* S7 (2): 1–9.

Garland, M., J. S. Morris, B. A. Rosner, M. J. Stampfer, V. L. Spate, C. J. Baskett, W. C. Willett, and D. J. Hunter. 1993. "Toenail Trace Element Levels as Biomarkers: Reproducibility Over a 6-Year Period." *Cancer Epidemiology and Prevention Biomarkers* 2 (5): 493–97.

Garrett, D. A., J. K. Sangha, M. T. Kothari, and D. Boyle. 2011. "Field-Friendly Techniques for Assessment of Biomarkers of Nutrition for Development." *American Journal of Clinical Nutrition* 94 (2): 685S–90S.

Holen, T., F. Norheim, T. E. Gundersen, P. Mitry, J. Linseisen, P. O. Iversen, and C. A. Drevon. 2016. "Biomarkers for Nutrient Intake with Focus on Alternative Sampling Techniques." *Genes & Nutrition* 11 (1): Article 12.

Jaszczak, A., K. Lundeen, and S. Smith. 2009. "Using Nonmedically Trained Interviewers to Collect Biomeasures in a National In-Home Survey." *Field Methods* 21 (1): 26–48.

Kakkar, P., and F. N. Jaffery. 2005. "Biological Markers for Metal Toxicity." *Environmental Toxicology and Pharmacology* 19 (2): 335–49.

Lacher, D. A., L. E. Berman, T.-C. Chen, and K. S. Porter. 2013. "Comparison of Dried Blood Spot to Venous Methods for Hemoglobin A1c, Glucose, Total Cholesterol, High-Density Lipoprotein Cholesterol, and C-Reactive Protein." *Clinica Chimica Acta* 422: 54–58.

Langer, E. K., K. J. Johnson, M. M. Shafer, P. Gorski, J. Overdier, J. Musselman, and J. A. Ross. 2011. "Characterization of the Elemental Composition of Newborn Blood Spots Using Sector-Field Inductively Coupled Plasma-Mass Spectrometry." *Journal of Exposure Science and Environmental Epidemiology* 21 (4): 355–64.

McDade, T. W. 2014. "Development and Validation of Assay Protocols for Use with Dried Blood Spot Samples." *American Journal of Human Biology* 26 (1): 1–9.

McDade, T. W., S. Williams, and J. J. Snodgrass. 2007. "What a Drop Can Do: Dried Blood Spots as a Minimally Invasive Method for Integrating Biomarkers into Population-Based Research." *Demography* 44 (4): 899–925.

Mei, J. 2014. "Dried Blood Spot Sample Collection, Storage, and Transportation." In *Dried Blood Spots: Applications and Techniques*, edited by W. Li and M. S. Lee, 21–31. Hoboken, NJ: John Wiley & Sons.

Neufeld, L., A. García-Guerra, D. Sánchez-Francia, O. Newton-Sánchez, M. D. Ramírez-Villalobos, and J. Rivera-Dommarco. 2002. "Hemoglobin Measured by Hemocue and a Reference Method in Venous and Capillary Blood: A Validation Study." *Salud Pública de México* 44 (3): 219–27.

NRC (National Research Council). 2006. *Human Biomonitoring for Environmental Chemicals*. Washington, DC: National Academies Press.

Ostler, M. W., J. H. Porter, and O. M. Buxton. 2014. "Dried Blood Spot Collection of Health Biomarkers to Maximize Participation in Population Studies." *Journal of Visualized Experiments* 2014 (83): e50973.

Poblete-Naredo, I., and A. Albores. 2016. "Molecular Biomarkers to Assess Health Risks Due to Environmental Contaminants Exposure." *Biomédica* 36 (2): 309–35.

Samuelsson, L. B., M. H. Hall, S. McLean, J. H. Porter, L. Berkman, M. Marino, G. Sembajwe, T. W. McDade, and O. M. Buxton. 2015. "Validation of Biomarkers of CVD Risk from Dried Blood Spots in Community-Based Research: Methodologies and Study-Specific Serum Equivalencies." *Biodemography and Social Biology* 61 (3): 285–97.

Sanchis-Gomar, F., J. Cortell-Ballester, H. Pareja-Galeano, G. Banfi, and G. Lippi. 2013. "Hemoglobin Point-of-Care Testing: The HemoCue System." *Journal of Laboratory Automation* 18 (3): 198–205.

Sanders, A. P., S. K. Miller, V. Nguyen, J. B. Kotch, and R. C. Fry. 2014. "Toxic Metal Levels in Children Residing in a Smelting Craft Village in Vietnam: A Pilot Biomonitoring Study." *BMC Public Health* 14 (1): Article 114.

Schindler, Birgit Karin, Marta Esteban, Holger Martin Koch, Argelia Castano, Stephan Koslitz, Ana Cañas, Ludwine Casteleyn, Marike Kolossa-Gehring, Gerda Schwedler, Greet Schoeters, Elly Den Hond, Ovnair Sepai, Karen Exley, Louis Bloemen, Milena Horvat, Lisbeth E. Knudsen, Anke Joas, Reinhard Joas, Pierre Biot, Dominique Aerts, Ana Lopez, Olga Huetos, Andromachi Katsonouri, Katja Maurer-Chronakis, Lucie Kasparova, Karel Vrbík, Peter Rudnai, Miklos Naray, Cedric Guignard, Marc E. Fischer, Danuta Ligocka, Beata Janasik, M. Fátima Reis, Sónia Namorado, Cristian Pop, Irina Dumitrascu, Katarina Halzlova, Eleonora

Fabianova, Darja Mazej, Janja Snoj Tratnik, Marika Berglund, Bo A. Jönsson, Andrea Lehmann, Pierre Crettaz, Hanne Frederiksen, Flemming Nielsen, Helena McGrath, Ian Nesbitt, Koen De Cremer, Guido Vanermen, Gudrun Koppen, Michael Wilhelm, Kerstin Becker, and Jürgen Angerer. 2014. "The European COPHES/DEMOCOPHES Project: Towards Transnational Comparability and Reliability of Human Biomonitoring Results." *International Journal of Hygiene and Environmental Health* 217 (6): 653–61.

Smolders, R., E. Den Hond, G. Koppen, E. Govarts, H. Willems, L. Casteleyn, M. Kolossa-Gehring, et al. 2015. "Interpreting Biomarker Data from the COPHES/DEMOCOPHES Twin Projects: Using External Exposure Data to Understand Biomarker Differences Among Countries." *Environmental Research* 141: 86–95.

Timmerman, P., S. White, Z. Cobb, R. de Vries, E. Thomas, and B. van Baar. 2013. "Update of the EBF Recommendation for the Use of DBS in Regulated Bioanalysis Integrating the Conclusions from the EBF DBS-Microsampling Consortium." *Bioanalysis* 5 (17): 2129–36.

Vimercati, L., A. Baldassarre, M. F. Gatti, T. Gagliardi, M. Serinelli, L. De Maria, A. Caputi, Angelica A. Dirodi, Ida Galise, Francesco Cuccaro, and Giorgio Assennato. 2016. "Non-Occupational Exposure to Heavy Metals of the Residents of an Industrial Area and Biomonitoring." *Environmental Monitoring and Assessment* 188 (12): Article 673.

Vimercati, L., F. Cuccaro, M. Serinelli, L. Bisceglia, I. Galise, M. Conversano, S. Minerba, A. Mincuzzi, T. Martino, M. A. Storelli, T. Gagliardi, and G. Assennato. 2013. "Exposure Assessment to Heavy Metals in General Population in a Polluted Area through Biological Monitoring." *E3S Web of Conferences* 1: Article 40005.

Were, F. H., W. Njue, J. Murungi, and R. Wanjau. 2008. "Use of Human Nails as Bio-Indicators of Heavy Metals Environmental Exposure Among School Age Children in Kenya." *Science of the Total Environment* 393 (2–3): 376–84.

WHO (World Health Organization). 2015. "Human Biomonitoring: Facts and Figures." Report, WHO Regional Office for Europe, Copenhagen.

ULAB AND OTHER RELEVANT STUDIES

Abdulkareem, J. H., A. Abdulkadir, and N. Abdu. 2015. "Vertical Distribution of Lead (Pb) in Farmlands Around Contaminated Goldmine in Zamfara State, Northern Nigeria." *African Journal of Agricultural Research* 10 (53): 4975–89.

Dowling, R., B. Ericson, J. Caravanos, P. Grigsby, and Y. Amoyaw-Osei. 2015. "Spatial Associations Between Contaminated Land and Socio Demographics in Ghana." *International Journal of Environmental Research and Public Health* 12 (10): 13587–601.

Dzomba, P., S. Nyoni, and N. Mudavanhu. 2012. "Heavy Metal Contamination Risk Through Consumption of Traditional Food Plants Growing Around Bindura Town, Zimbabwe." *Journal of Toxicology and Environmental Health Sciences* 4 (5): 92–95.

Ericson, B., J. Caravanos, K. Chatham-Stephens, P. Landrigan, and R. Fuller. 2013. "Approaches to Systematic Assessment of Environmental Exposures Posed at Hazardous Waste Sites in the Developing World: The Toxic Sites Identification Program." *Environmental Monitoring and Assessment* 185 (2): 1755–66.

Glorennec, P., J. P. Lucas, C. Mandin, and B. Le Bot. 2012. "French Children's Exposure to Metals Via Ingestion of Indoor Dust, Outdoor Playground Dust and Soil: Contamination Data." *Environment International* 45: 129–34.

Islam, M. S., M. K. Ahmed, and M. Habibullah-Al-Mamun. 2015. "Metal Speciation in Soil and Health Risk Due to Vegetables Consumption in Bangladesh." *Environmental Monitoring and Assessment* 187 (5): 288.

Khan, M. U., R. N. Malik, and S. Muhammad. 2013. "Human Health Risk from Heavy Metal Via Food Crops Consumption with Wastewater Irrigation Practices in Pakistan." *Chemosphere* 93 (10): 2230–8.

Mbilu, Z. J., and M. E. Lyimo. 2015. "Heavy Metals Contamination in Soils and Selected Edible Parts of Free-Range Local Chicken." *International Journal of Environmental Science and Technology* 12 (4): 1409–14.

Muhanji, G., R. L. Roothaert, C. Webo, and M. Stanley. 2011. "African Indigenous Vegetable Enterprises and Market Access for Small-Scale Farmers in East Africa." *International Journal of Agricultural Sustainability* 9 (1): 194–202.

Oguri, T., G. Suzuki, H. Matsukami, N. Uchida, N. M. Tue, P. H. Viet, S. Takahashi, S. Tanabe, and H. Takigami. 2017. "Exposure Assessment of Heavy Metals in an E-Waste Processing Area in Northern Vietnam." *Science of The Total Environment* 621: 1115–23. doi:10.1016/j .scitotenv.2017.10.115.

Okoye, C. O., C. N. Ibeto, and J. N. Ihedioha. 2011. "Assessment of Heavy Metals in Chicken Feeds Sold in South Eastern, Nigeria." *Advances in Applied Science Research* 2 (3): 63–68.

Olowoyo, J. O., L. L. Mugivhisa, and Z. G. Magoloi. 2016. "Composition of Trace Metals in Dust Samples Collected from Selected High Schools in Pretoria, South Africa." *Applied and Environmental Soil Science* 2016 (14): 1–9. doi:10.1155/2016/5829657.

Secretariat of the Basel Convention and the United National Environment Programme. 2003. *Technical Guidelines for the Environmentally Sound Management of Waste Lead-Acid Batteries.* Basel Convention Series/SBC No. 2003/9, accessed January 2020, http://archive .basel.int/pub/techguid/tech-wasteacid.pdf

Tirima, S., C. Bartrem, I. von Lindern, M. von Braun, D. Lind, S. M. Anka, and A. Abdullahi. 2018. "Food Contamination as a Pathway for Lead Exposure in Children During the 2010–2013 Lead Poisoning Epidemic in Zamfara, Nigeria." *Journal of Environmental Sciences.* 67: 260–72.

WHO (World Health Organization). *Recycling Used Lead-Acid Batteries: Health Considerations.* ISBN: 978-92-4-151285-5, accessed December 2017, http://www.who.int/ipcs/publications /ulab/en/

Zheng, J., K. H. Chen, X. Yan, S. J. Chen, G. C. Hu, X. W. Peng, J. G. Yuan, B. X. Mai, and Z. Y. Yang. 2013. "Heavy Metals in Food, House Dust, and Water from an E-Waste Recycling Area in South China and the Potential Risk to Human Health." *Ecotoxicology and Environmental Safety* 96: 205–12.

METHODS

The sources listed here cover only the peer-reviewed literature (as opposed to guidance); bioaccessibility / bioavailability. For a complete official methods compilation, see "Hazardous Waste Methods / SW-846" (https://www.epa.gov /hw-sw846) and "Collection of Methods" (https://www.epa.gov /measurements-modeling/collection-methods) on the US Environmental Protection Agency (EPA) website.

Brent, R. N., H. Wines, J. Luther, N. Irving, J. Collins, and D. L. Drake. 2017. "Validation of Handheld X-Ray Fluorescence for *In Situ* Measurement of Mercury in Soils." *Journal of Environmental Chemical Engineering* 5 (1): 768–76.

Chirila, E., and C. Draghici. 2011. "Analytical Approaches for Sampling and Sample Preparation for Heavy Metals Analysis in Biological Materials." In *Environmental Heavy Metal Pollution and Effects on Child Mental Development: Risk Assessment and Prevention Strategies,* edited by L. I. Simeonov, M. V. Kochubovski, and B. G. Simeonova, 129–43. Dordrecht, The Netherlands: Springer.

Cornelis, R., B. Heinzow, R. F. Herber, J. M. Christensen, O. M. Poulsen, E. Sabbioni, D. M. Templeton, Y. Thomassen, M. Vahter, and O. Vesterberg. 1995. "Sample Collection Guidelines for Trace Elements in Blood and Urine (Technical Report)." *Pure and Applied Chemistry* 67 (8–9): 1575–608.

Cornelis, R., B. Heinzow, R. F. Herber, J. M. Christensen, O. M. Poulsen, E. Sabbioni, D. M. Templeton, Y. Thomassen, M. Vahter, and O. Vesterberg. 1996. "Sample Collection Guidelines for Trace Elements in Blood and Urine." *Journal of Trace Elements in Medicine and Biology* 10 (2): 103–27.

Griffin, R. M. 1986. "Biological Monitoring for Heavy Metals: Practical Concerns." *Journal of Occupational and Environmental Medicine* 28 (8): 615–58.

Ianni, C., A. Bignasca, N. Calace, P. Rivaro, and E. Magi. "Bioaccessibility of Metals in Soils: Comparison between Chemical Extractions and *In Vitro* Tests." 2014. *Chemistry and Ecology* 30 (6): 541–54.

Ibanez, Y., B. Le Bot, and P. Glorennec. 2010. "House-Dust Metal Content and Bioaccessibility: A Review." *European Journal of Mineralogy* 22 (5): 629–37.

Jobanputra, N. K., R. Jones, G. Buckler, R. P. Cody, M. Gochfeld, T. M. Matte, D. Q. Rich, and G. G. Rhoads. 1998. "Accuracy and Reproducibility of Blood Lead Testing in Commercial Laboratories." *Archives of Pediatrics & Adolescent Medicine* 152 (6): 548–53.

Juhasz, A. L., E. Smith, C. Nelson, D. J. Thomas, and K. Bradham. 2014. "Variability Associated with As *In Vivo–In Vitro* Correlations When Using Different Bioaccessibility Methodologies." *Environmental Science & Technology* 48 (19): 11646–53.

Kummrow, F., F. F. Silva, R. Kuno, A. L. Souza, and P. V. Oliveira. 2008. "Biomonitoring Method for the Simultaneous Determination of Cadmium and Lead in Whole Blood by Electrothermal Atomic Absorption Spectrometry for Assessment of Environmental Exposure." *Talanta* 75 (1): 246–52.

Le Bot, B., J.-P. Lucas, F. Lacroix, and P. Glorennec. 2016. "Exposure of Children to Metals via Tap Water Ingestion at Home: Contamination and Exposure Data from a Nationwide Survey in France." *Environment International* 94: 500–507.

Li, J., K. Li, X.-Y. Cui, N. T. Basta, L.-P. Li, H.-B. Li, and L. Q. Ma. 2015. "*In Vitro* Bioaccessibility and *In Vivo* Relative Bioavailability in 12 Contaminated Soils: Method Comparison and Method Development." *Science of the Total Environment* 532: 812–20.

Ljung, K., A. Oomen, M. Duits, O. Selinus, and M. Berglund. 2007. "Bioaccessibility of Metals in Urban Playground Soils." *Journal of Environmental Science and Health Part A* 42 (9): 1241–50.

Oomen, A. G., A. Hack, M. Minekus, E. Zeijdner, C. Cornelis, G. Schoeters, W. Verstraete, Tom Van de Wiele, Joanna Wragg, Cathy J. M. Rompelberg, Adriënne J. A. M. Sips, and Joop H. Van Wijnen. 2002. "Comparison of Five *In Vitro* Digestion Models to Study the Bioaccessibility of Soil Contaminants." *Environmental Science & Technology* 36 (15): 3326–34.

Oomen, A. G., C. J. Rompelberg, M. A. Bruil, C. J. Dobbe, D. P. Pereboom, and A. J. Sips. 2003. "Development of an *In Vitro* Digestion Model for Estimating the Bioaccessibility of Soil Contaminants." *Archives of Environmental Contamination and Toxicology* 44 (3): 281–87.

Peijnenburg, W. J., M. Zablotskaja, and M. G. Vijver. 2007. "Monitoring Metals in Terrestrial Environments within a Bioavailability Framework and a Focus on Soil Extraction." *Ecotoxicology and Environmental Safety* 67 (2): 163–79.

Sheppard, B. S., D. T. Heitkemper, and C. M. Gaston. 1994. "Microwave Digestion for the Determination of Arsenic, Cadmium and Lead in Seafood Products by Inductively Coupled Plasma Atomic Emission and Mass Spectrometry." *Analyst* 119 (8): 1683–86.

Turner, A., and K. H. Ip. 2007. "Bioaccessibility of Metals in Dust from the Indoor Environment: Application of a Physiologically Based Extraction Test." *Environmental Science & Technology* 41 (22): 7851–56.

Sampling design

EPA (US Environmental Protection Agency). 2002. "Guidance on Choosing a Sampling Design for Environmental Data Collection for Use in Developing a Quality Assurance Plan." Guidance document, EPA, Washington, DC. https://www.epa.gov/sites/production/files/2015-06/documents/g5s-final.pdf.

Systematic grid sampling versus stratified random sampling

Gilbert, R. O., and B. A. Pulsipher. 2005. "Role of Sampling Designs in Obtaining Representative Data." *Environmental Forensics* 6 (1): 27–33.

Mattuck, R., R. Blanchet, and A. D. Wait. 2005. "Data Representativeness for Risk Assessment." *Environmental Forensics* 6 (1): 65–70.

PNNL (Pacific Northwest National Laboratory). n.d. "Visual Sample Plan." Software tool, PNNL, Richland, WA. https://vsp.pnnl.gov/.

Ramsey, C. A., and A. D. Hewitt. 2005. "A Methodology for Assessing Sample Representativeness." *Environmental Forensics* 6 (1): 71–75.

Zhu, A. X., J. Liu, F. Du, S. J. Zhang, C. Z. Qin, J. Burt, T. Behrens, and T. Scholten. 2015. "Predictive Soil Mapping with Limited Sample Data." *European Journal of Soil Science* 66 (3): 535–47.